WHAT PEOPLE ARE SAYING ...

"*Grantepreneur* is a new and refreshingly encouraging book, a must buy for anyone who has dreamed of getting started in a grant career and business! The author, a highly regarded colleague and leader in the grants industry, has written a book that drills down to Basic Grants 101 information, incorporating how we can discover our cause and provide grant services in our communities. There are so many relevant pointers and resources, that I whole-heartedly recommend this book for anyone considering becoming a grant consultant, and for educators teaching others about grants and how to make your way in the industry. I especially liked the chapter on Making Meaning and Money as a Grant Professional. *Grantepreneur* will be a recommended reference for my online students because it fully answers all of the questions that I'm asked on a daily basis. Bravo and gratitude to Katherine for writing this book and guiding the way!"

Dr. Beverly A. Browning, CSPF
Author of *Grant Writing for Dummies* and *Perfect Phrases for Writing Grant Proposals*
Online Instructor, Workshop Presenter, Coach & Motivational Speaker at http://bevbrowning.com/

***

"*Grantepreneur* is a unique book that I will reference for many years to come. When individuals ask me about getting involved in the world of philanthropy, this is undoubtedly the number one resource I will recommend. Well written. Easy to follow. And so very, very practical."

Cynthia M. Adams, CEO, GrantStation.com, Inc.
Member Women in Philanthropy

***

"*Grantepreneur* is a clear, supportive guide for those considering a career in grant proposal development. Katherine Heart defines the work of grants professional then leads you through a series of self-assessment and planning steps to help you achieve both personal satisfaction and career success."

Barbara Floersch, Executive Director, The Grantsmanship Center
Author of Grantsmanship: Program Planning and Proposal Writing

***

"*Grantepreneur* is a combination of business planning guide, life decision tool and workbook that leads you through the process of deciding about grantwriting as a career. It's thoughtful and action oriented, asking philosophical, practical and financial questions and helping you answer them for your individual situation. I'll definitely recommend this book to people who come to me for career advice."

Michael Wells, GPC, CFRE
Author: *Strategic Grantseeking, Understanding Nonprofit Finances, Successful Program Evaluation*
Past Board Member: Grant Professionals Association and Grant Professionals Certification Institute
Owner (Retired) Grants Northwest

***

"I was immediately drawn to this book, not only because of the cool title, but as a result of my love for the grant profession and the business of grants. The draw did not disappoint! The author effortlessly communicates well in both the acronym filled grant-speak world and in the language of business! The book is a practical guide giving readers tangible tools, career instruction, and a business road-map to success."

Danny W. Blitch II, MPA, GPC, Organizing Editor and Co-Author of *Prepare for the GPC Exam: Earn Your Grant Professional Certified Credential*

***

"In *Grantepreneur,* Katherine F.H. Heart offers a wealth of valuable information, comprehensive resources and unique insights into the "World of Grants." As an expert in grant consulting and proposal writing, Heart offers a realistic and encouraging overview of what it takes to channel passion and talent into a career that promotes critical social causes. *Grantepreneur* is a must read for anyone considering a new grant career or business as well as seasoned grant professionals who desire to advance to higher levels of success."

Rosemary Hanrahan, M.D., M.P.H.
Author of When Dreams Touch and Nonprofit Coach, Consultant, Grant Writer & Storyteller at www.beyondwordswellnessresources.com

***

"As a Development Consultant and Capacity Building Coach, volunteers often ask for my advice on how to identify potential funders and write a grant proposal. I look forward to recommending this book to them and am hopeful it will lead to more efficient use of resources and additional funding for essential causes in Illinois and across the country."

Gayle L. Nelson, Esq.
Development Consultant, Contributor to *NPQ Newswire,* Commissioner of the Illinois State Commission for the Elimination of Poverty

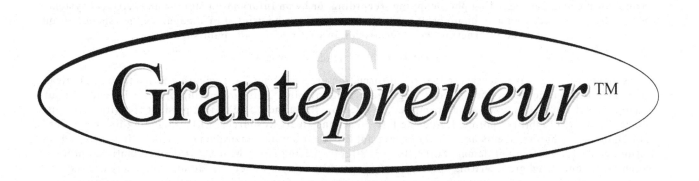

Getting Started in a Grant Career and Business

Katherine F.H. Heart, GPC, M.Ed.

Red Engine Press
Pittsburgh, PA
Printed in the United States.

DEDICATION

This book is dedicated to:

Bernadette M. Furin, MSW, M.Div., in gratitude for many years of personal support of my writing career and grant business.

Thanks to:

Jan Glick, M.S., CEO of Big Brothers Big Sisters of Greater Pittsburgh, my first grant client and mentor.

Colleagues in the Grant Professionals Association and Dena Hartigan for her thoughtful feedback on this manuscript.

Participants in my Grant Career and Business seminars for generously sharing their personal and professional challenges.

CONTENTS

ABOUT THE AUTHOR

Katherine F.H. Heart, GPC, M.Ed., President of Heart Resources, LLC, received her Master of Education degree from the University of Pittsburgh in 1984. A graduate course in Grant Writing and Fundraising launched her into a lifetime of dedicated service to the nonprofit sector. Katherine developed, marketed and managed nonprofit fitness, health promotion and mental health training programs for 15 years. She was a certified advocate and training manager at two leading victim services agencies. She published creative non-fiction articles and in her late forties, Katherine became a technical writer and product development manager for a psychology consulting firm.

She has completed more than 200 hours of continuing education in technical writing, grant research, grant proposal writing, and budgeting with leading national trainers such as The Grantsmanship Center Inc., the Foundation Center of New York, and grant author Dr. Beverly Browning. Katherine founded Heart Resources, LLC in 2005. Her company provides grant services to improve quality of life in Western Pennsylvania (see www.heartresources.net).

Katherine is a member of the Grant Professionals Association (GPA), and was Founding President of the GPA-Western Pennsylvania Chapter. Katherine has earned the Grant Professional Certified (GPC) credential from the Grant Professional Certification Institute and was the first person to be recognized as a GPA Approved Trainer. Grant*epreneur*™ is her second book.

INTRODUCTION

Do you enjoy writing and care about a special cause? Are you yearning to be involved in improving your community? Are you seeking a meaningful career with flexibility and financial potential? Whether you are a new graduate or seasoned professional, the grants field offers growing career and business opportunities that will enable you to play a vital role. Grant research, proposal development and writing, and grant management skills are in demand at nonprofit organizations, government agencies, universities, hospitals, and for-profits occupied with finding funding for programs and services. Channel your passion by becoming a grant professional for your cause and community!

My career move into the grants field occurred about 15 years ago. I started as part-time freelancer (also known as a "sole proprietor" for a business owned and operated by an individual) to try out the work. I found that I loved writing grant proposals and was very good at winning funding. I started Heart Resources, LLC, which has grown into a successful regional grant specialty company. In 2008, I began presenting grant trainings, including grant career and business seminars to assist people in finding out how to get started and succeed in the grant profession.

This book grew from my own "lessons learned" in daily work with grant seeking organizations, and from listening to my colleagues and seminar participants. This is the first full-blown career guide for grant writing that offers similar topics as career books for other professions. It provides information that I wish was readily available when I started. No prior knowledge is required to read and understand this book. It is organized in a workbook format with engaging information about the World of Grants and the role of grant professionals, occupational options, the learning curve, ethics, and job growth projections. I ask thought-provoking personal and professional questions that will enable you to explore your interests, along with the meaningfulness and financial prospects of this career path. The various exercises were tested by seminar participants and colleagues. I'm excited to share the Grant Career Action Plan, which provides activities to take you through 10 Steps to Get Hired (and Re-Hired) for grant jobs. In the last chapter my 10 Grant*epreneur*™ Strategies will introduce you to the issues to consider when starting a freelance practice. The Resources section has an excellent array of websites, books, organizations, and training to explore.

My definition of a "Grant*epreneur*™" is "an individual who applies both grant competency and entrepreneurial skills to advance their cause, community and career or business." By definition, grants include the concept of benefit to the public and society. In myself and colleagues, I've observed that caring and passionate people with various skills and prior experiences are drawn (accidentally or on purpose) to develop their grant seeking abilities in order to bring much-needed funding for programs and services that help others. The Grant*epreneur*™ career and business model takes the purpose of grants into consideration through social enterprise and community-oriented business concepts, and does not promote incompatible big business practices. It will help you to explore whether the grant career path is right for you, but doesn't guarantee success. You will find more information at http://www.grantepreneur.com.

Skilled grant proposal writers are in high demand, but the World of Grants is competitive! You deserve plenty of information to make an educated decision. I want you to know what it takes to get started and be in a position to advance to higher levels of success. Grant*epreneur*™ will give you an insider's view of the opportunities, requirements and rewards, and concrete action steps and strategies to get ready, trained and hired for the grant profession.

As you read this book, I invite you to focus on finding your own answer to this question: "Is grant writing your next career or business?"

ONE

THE WORLD OF GRANTS

Professionals who work with grants find our careers and lives organized around the cycles of researching, writing and submitting, implementing, monitoring and reporting on grant-funded projects. This chapter will share that perspective and provide a personal tour of the "who, what, where, when, and why" of grants. The World of Grants is part of the broader philanthropic universe. The information provided here is an introduction and there is a wealth of resources for in-depth study at the end of this book.

What Is a Grant?

The grants field has its own "jargon" (words with a special or technical meaning) used specifically in grant proposals. We will use the following general terms and definitions throughout the book:

A GRANT is a financial award from a government agency or charitable organization to assist a recipient tax-exempt organization to carry out a public purpose. Grants are given for a designated time period to attain specific results. A grant is different from a contract or loan. Grants do not have to be repaid as long as the funds are used for the agreed upon purpose. Grants are not "free"—a written proposal, results, and reporting are required!

A GRANT PROPOSAL or GRANT APPLICATION is the formal written plan that requests funding.

A GRANT MAKER or FUNDER is the organization offering funding, typically through an established application process.

A GRANT SEEKER, APPLICANT, or RECIPIENT is the organization that requests and is eligible to receive grants.

A GRANT WRITER is the person who prepares grant guidelines on behalf of the funder, while GRANT PROPOSAL WRITER is the person who develops and writes grant proposals for applicants. A GRANT PROFESSIONAL utilizes a number of skills to prepare and manage grants. This is a growing profession and distinctions are not yet made by employers or the public. This book presents common information to get you started and may take you to any of these roles, so all of the above terms will be used here.

Who Gives Grants?

All of the major sectors utilize grants to some extent and employ grant professionals:

☐ The public sector exists to organize and carry out government-funded services including major infrastructure, health and safety, and other necessary services.

☐ The private sector of business and industry enables individuals to profit from inventing and producing products and services, along with participating as an investor.

☐ The nonprofit sector—also referred to as the "third sector"—provides need-based services and products with the purpose of improving human, social, and environmental conditions.

Grants provide a planned investment of funding within and between sectors for new and continuing projects, programs, and services that benefit the public. Grant-making organizations develop guidelines, assess applications, and distribute grant funding to eligible organizations for activities that promote the broader good rather than individual profit. Some of the taxes and charitable dollars that Americans give each year are later awarded as grants. Individuals of all income levels routinely donate money, goods, and time to agencies that serve others in need, while wealthier individuals may establish foundations or charitable trusts that give grants to improve their communities. Each type of grant maker has a unique reason to give grants.

☐ Local, state, and federal government gives contracts, loans, and grants from tax proceeds—our money—to fund programs and services that benefit the public. Congress appropriates funding for various public purposes. Funding is dispensed by twenty-six federal agencies with more than 1,500 grant making programs.

☐ Private, public, and community foundations are categories of charitable nonprofit organizations that offer grant funding to other nonprofit agencies that provide direct programs and services. Operating foundations provide funding for their own charitable activities. Foundations are usually created from individual or family wealth. A check of the business and family history of many municipalities in America is likely to turn up family foundations that continue to distribute funding from the wealth of past generations.

- Federations, or federated funds, are a joint fundraising effort by a nonprofit "umbrella" organization that distributes the contributions from individual donors (such as employees at workplaces) via grants to nonprofit agencies. Examples are the United Way, United Jewish Federation, and the United Negro College Fund.

- Corporations bestow a small portion of their profits as grants to causes and organizations that are aligned with their business, which enhances public relations. Company foundations and giving programs may offer grants to organizations in which their employees are involved.

Who Receives Grants?

- State and county governments can apply for federal grants, and then sub-grant (redistribute) monies through grants to nonprofits and smaller municipalities.

- Companies and small businesses can be eligible for research, development, and technology grants for projects that will eventually benefit the public.

- Nonprofit organizations are major grant recipients since their purpose embraces a broader good over personal profit. There are more than one million nonprofit organizations in the United States as confirmed by registration and approval from the IRS for tax-exempt status. Nearly half of the nonprofits in the United States are located in seven states (California, Florida, Illinois, New York, Ohio, Pennsylvania, and Texas). Nonprofit organizations are eligible to apply for grants from corporations, foundations, United Way, and also federal, state, and local governments.

- Small community-level grassroots groups can receive grants under the fiscal sponsorship of an IRS-sanctioned nonprofit organization. There are countless unregistered community groups in the United States.

- Individuals can seek funding for educational purposes in the form of scholarships and fellowships. University researchers, faculty and doctoral students often apply for grants to further their work in medical research, the arts, and other academic areas.

Individual members of the general public do not often receive grants for personal use unless they are financially eligible and are experiencing other problems.

Drug discounts and donated medications are given to patients with financial hardship by foundations run by pharmaceutical companies. Individuals may qualify for subsidies to help with utility bills that are promoted as "grants." A small number of nonprofit organizations provide "cash grants" directly to families who are experiencing extreme hardship and have nowhere else to turn. There is careful scrutiny of financial assets and an application is required.

One example of a grant given to individuals is the National Multiple Sclerosis Foundation Brighter Tomorrow Grant, which provides people who have been diagnosed with MS specific goods or services (valued up to $1,000 per recipient) to improve their quality of life. Individuals who apply for this particular grant must not have any other means of fulfilling their requested need.[1] All grant applications involve completing forms. The Foundation Center of New York publishes the *Foundation Grants to Individuals* directory.

Grant writing is only one of many sources of funding for nonprofit programs and services. Volunteers and professional fundraisers seek charitable gifts of money, goods, and services from throughout the community. The financial and "in-kind" (non-monetary) donations come from different sources. Each nonprofit organization determines the right mix of resources needed to sustain their work.

Resources for Nonprofit Organizations — Other than Grants:

- Planned giving and major gifts from wealthy donors

- Smaller donations of time, goods, and money from individuals, groups and companies

- Capital campaigns to find money for big needs such as new facilities

- Investment income from endowments

- Social enterprise, internal profit centers, partnerships with business

- Phone and letter appeals

- Special events

- Fees charged for programs, services, memberships

- Sales of goods and products

- Contracts from government to deliver services

Be aware that you may encounter plenty of misinformation and myths about how much grants can do for an organization. Grant writers must avoid wishful thinking and not make the mistake of imagining that grants will be able to start a nonprofit or be the only source of funding, raise ongoing operating support, make or break the agency budget, or save the agency from a dire financial situation. Funders dislike being placed in the role of rescuer and they can detect these scenarios by reviewing the proposal and budget. A Development Plan with multiple sources of revenue in which grants are part of the mix is the best practice.

1 Information obtained from http://msfocus.org/Brighter-Tomorrow-Grant.aspx

What Is the Grant Proposal Writer's Role?

Grant proposal writing is a technical writing skill rather than an art form genre like fiction or poetry. It requires not only strong English writing skills, but also knowledge of proposal formats and terminology. It is helpful to have a general knowledge or experience in project planning and spreadsheet budgets. The primary responsibility is to prepare proposals that make the organization's best case for funding, meeting both the funder's requirements and the organization's plans to work on a problem. An interesting and challenging aspect of writing an effective "winning" grant proposal is to add persuasive points that engage the funder's interest and "sells" the proposed project. Later in this chapter you will be able to view an actual grant proposal. First, let's look at the role and related tasks in greater detail.

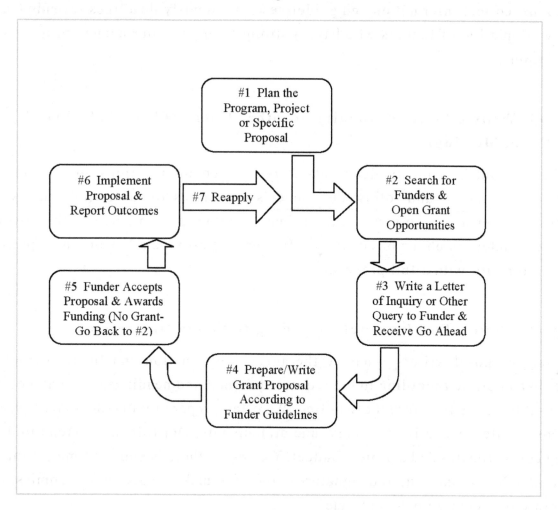

Grant Seeking Process

Step #1: Plan the Program, Project or Proposal

Prior to starting a grant proposal, we must become familiar with the organization, especially the long-range plans, and current programs and budget details. We gather information from various sources such as: authorized documents (strategic plans, annual reports, past grant proposals and reports); websites; annual plans; interviews with staff; and participant input. We may help agencies to assess the need for new projects, and develop pre-proposals that facilitate discussion with funders.

Step #2: Search for Funders and Open Grant Opportunities

We conduct Internet-based research to find grants, learn about grantmaking organizations, collect information and guidelines, and identify deadlines for submission. We develop a list of funders who have a strong interest in our agency programs and populations.

Step #3: Write a Letter of Inquiry, or other Query (Phone Call, Email, On-line Form, Meeting)

We find out how the funder wants to receive communications and requests for grant consideration, and follow the funder's guidelines for an initial inquiry. The proposal writer may also serve as the primary contact person between the organization and funder via phone or email. The funder will provide a Yes or No response on moving forward with a full proposal.

Step #4: Write a Full Proposal According to Funder Guidelines

Grant proposal writers assemble the agency information and funder guidelines, develop an outline according to the requested format and headings, write and edit the proposal to be ready before the deadline. We often prepare related documents such as the cover letter, executive summary, and attachments. Our role may extend to developing cost estimates and a project budget. We ensure there is enough time for internal reviews, editing, and required signatures, and then make a successful submission by or before the required date and time.

Grant proposals range in complexity and length:

- ☐ Online Application Forms
- ☐ Letters of Inquiry/Intent (1-3 pages)

- [ ] Short Letter Proposals (3-5 pages)

- [ ] Local Foundation Proposals (5-15 pages)

- [ ] National Foundations, United Way, and Government Applications (15 pages and up)

Step #5: Funder Accepts Proposal and Awards Funding

We may develop a thank you letter acknowledging that the agency has received the grant monies, but an official representative (CEO, Executive Director, or Board Chair) must sign the letter. Funders require a signed contract that obligates the agency to fulfill the proposal or risk returning grant monies.

Step #6: Implement Proposal and Report Outcomes

After the grant award is made, an agency must use the money according to the agreed upon plan put forth in the proposal. Grant projects are time-limited and the proposal writer may also be responsible for submitting the agency's report on the use of grant money and project outcomes at the end of the funding period. It is prudent to monitor how well the proposal is implemented in case there are problems and further discussion is required with the funder. Project management may be completed by other staff but the proposal writer will be better prepared for reporting if we check the progress being made.

Step # 7: Reapply for Funding

Funders can choose to award grants in subsequent years upon review of reported results and submission of another proposal. We often help to cultivate and maintain relationships that increase the chance of future funding.

At small to medium-size nonprofit agencies, grants may be combined with related duties such as writing for a website, annual reports, press releases, and fundraising letters. You may be responsible for, or expected to pitch in with, other fundraising activities. Larger organizations hire grant specialists and managers to develop full-scale plans for complex grant requests to national foundations and government agencies. Pursuing many grants and/or larger grants is a continuous process involving researching, planning, writing, budgeting, submitting, tracking, and reporting for grant proposals.

Complex applications demand an intermediate to advanced level of professional knowledge, skill, and experience. Expert level grant proposal writing is one of the most valuable and in-demand professional writing skills in both the private and public sectors.

In the current highly competitive funding environment, grant writing has grown into a separate specialization, as evidenced by the development of national associations that offer professional development programs at local chapters, training workshops and webinars, and certification exams.

What Exactly Do Grant Writers Write?

Each proposal is tailored to the funder's guidelines and may appear to be very different from other proposals; however, there are similar components among all proposals that describe the organization, problem and need, purpose of the proposal, expected outcomes and evaluation, sustainability, and budget. A cover letter and executive summary may be required to introduce the narrative and budget sections. Several attachments are routinely requested such as the organization's tax exemption letter, list of board members, support letters, job descriptions, and other documents.

My Favorite Grant Proposal

In 2005, I had a chance conversation with an army reservist who was home on leave from the Iraq War. What I heard about the real problem of post-traumatic stress was alarming. I was a grant writer for an agency that provided a hotline and referrals for people in crisis. Having knowledge of the available services enabled me to identify an unmet need and assist the agency to develop a hotline service that could help returning combatants and their families to receive support and referrals well before there was widespread public awareness.

In the grant writer's role, I researched and identified a funder. I conducted phone interviews with mental health therapists working for the Veterans Administration, along with gaining a letter of support and cooperation from the county VA administrator. I learned more about the barriers to awareness, disclosure, and treatment. I worked with both the agency and VA officials to develop a collaborative agreement for the application. I worked with agency staff to design the outreach program and hotline service. I wrote the proposal and worked with the Executive Director to develop a realistic budget.

This is one of my favorite grant proposals because the agency allowed me to take a leading role in developing the project. It was challenging to write a persuasive and complete proposal within this funder's strict guidelines. It was meaningful to find funding for this program benefiting military members and families, since I grew up in a military family and knew about PTSD. The sample grant shown on the following pages illustrates how a well-written brief proposal can result in start-up funding to serve a vital need in the community. A one-year grant of $47,000 was awarded by the American Psychiatric Foundation. Some details and names have been changed to protect individual identities.

Proposal to the American Psychiatric Foundation

Submitted by CRISIS Pittsburgh

"Outreach and Education towards a Public 800 Hotline for

Early Intervention of PTSD in Service Combatants

Returning from the Middle East"

Executive Summary

CRISIS Pittsburgh is a nonprofit 501(c)3 IRS tax exempt organization with the mission of offering immediate emotional support by telephone volunteers trained to help people who may be suicidal, in emotional distress, or in need of reassurance, information or referrals.

CRISIS Pittsburgh has become aware of more than 3,200 National Guard and Reservists in Greater Pittsburgh and Western Pennsylvania who have completed one or more tours of duty in the Middle East. Up to 40% of returning soldiers will develop some form of Post-Traumatic Stress Disorder (PTSD), according to the Allegheny County Director of Veteran's Affairs. However, many service members are reluctant to disclose symptoms because the stigma attached to a mental illness could affect their jobs, service records, and ability to redeploy with their fellow soldiers.

Working closely with regional Veteran's Administration collaborators, CRISIS Pittsburgh proposes to develop and initiate an Outreach and Education Campaign. We will hire a veteran with first-hand awareness and treatment experience for public speaking engagements at Reserve and Guard Units to help reduce the stigma of PTSD among soldiers. In the coming year, the Campaign will provide information to approximately 3,200 soldiers and their families about the signs and symptoms of post-traumatic stress. CRISIS Pittsburgh and VA professionals will provide training about PTSD to our hotline volunteers that will enable them to deliver phone information, support and community resources.

Further, CRISIS Pittsburgh will collaborate with Veteran's Administration officials and an evaluator from the University of Pittsburgh's Graduate School of Public Health to gather data and information about the outcomes of the Campaign and feasibility of creating a nationally-accessible 800 24-hour hotline for returning combatants and their families. The deliverables from the project will be packaged for dissemination to other crisis hotlines across the United States.

CRISIS Pittsburgh respectfully requests a grant in the amount of $47,000 to assist the agency in developing, implementing and evaluating this project from July 1, 2006 to June 30, 2007.

Proposal to the American Psychiatric Foundation
Submitted by CRISIS Pittsburgh

*"Outreach and Education towards a Public 800 Hotline for Early Intervention
of PTSD in Service Combatants Returning from the Middle East"*

Organizational Background

CRISIS Pittsburgh is a volunteer-based, 501(c)3 IRS tax exempt nonprofit organization with a mission to offer immediate emotional support by telephone volunteers trained to help people of all ages who may be suicidal, in emotional distress, or in need of reassurance, information, or referral services. Our agency has 34 years of experience in providing multiple telephone support services, and 100 volunteer telephone workers answer over 20,000 calls yearly for youth, adults, and senior citizens, and provide community education and training services. CRISIS Pittsburgh is one of the largest of 55 CRISIS Centers affiliated with CRISIS USA, and the only hotline in the region that is accredited by the American Association of Suicidology.

Problem and Need

At CRISIS Pittsburgh, we are aware of the many service personnel returning from combat in Iraq and Afghanistan. At least 9,000 Pennsylvania National Guard and Reserve soldiers have seen combat in Afghanistan and Iraq. More than 26,000 Guard and Reserve soldiers from Pennsylvania have served in one or both areas in some capacity. In Allegheny County alone, approximately 3,200 Reservists (many of whom have completed more than one tour of duty) have served in the Middle East.

According to Rob Conrad, the Allegheny County Director of Veteran's Affairs, up to 40% of returning soldiers have some form of Post-Traumatic Stress Disorder (PTSD). He has acknowledged that soldiers are reluctant to disclose PTSD symptoms because they are afraid the stigma of a mental health condition will follow them to their employment and risk their jobs, and result in separation from their "buddies" in the event of redeployment. This second reason for not disclosing PTSD symptoms was confirmed by CRISIS Pittsburgh in confidential interviews with recently returned enlisted soldiers who saw 18 months or more of combat action in Iraq.

CRISIS Pittsburgh completed a feasibility study to determine the need to establish a public confidential and anonymous toll-free hotline for returning combatants and their families. We have made inquiries as to whether the hotline would be an acceptable alternative to contacting the local Veterans Administration treatment system. We conferred with James Brock, an Outreach Counseling Technician (who has seen combat in Iraq as an officer), and his supervisor, Al Blake, a licensed psychologist and PTSD expert at our county's Veteran's Outreach Counseling Center, as well as Dale Zorn, the Clinical Coordinator of the PTSD Team at the Veteran's Administration Hospital in Pittsburgh.

While each expert indicated that services are available through the Veteran's Administration, they agreed that there is a need for outreach and education to de-stigmatize PTSD among the more than 100 Guard and Reserve Units in Western Pennsylvania. They were in support of a toll-free number where soldiers and their families who were not predisposed to contact the V.A. could turn to for information, support and referral. All were interested in developing a collaborative relationship with CRISIS Pittsburgh to train volunteers, and as a referral resource.

Goals, Objectives and Activities

The target audience for this project is National Guard and Reserve Unit soldiers and their families in Pittsburgh, Allegheny County and Southwestern PA areas with high deployment rates. We will reach more than 100 Units and 3,200 soldiers and their families. The following charts show the goals, objectives and key activities, personnel and hours of effort for the one-year period from July 1, 2006 to June 30, 2007.

Goal 1: Develop and implement an Outreach and Education Campaign that de-stigmatizes PTSD, addresses signs and symptoms, and offers hotline resources to National Guard and Reserve Units in Western PA.

Objective 1.1: Provide speaking engagements, develop and distribute a pocket-size booklet to 3,200 soldiers.

Activities	Staff	Jul	Aug	Sep	Oct	Nov	Dec	Jan	Feb	Mar	Apr	May	Jun
1.1.a Develop copy for booklet about signs/help for PTSD.	VA Writer	4 9	4 9										
1.1.b Print booklet.	Printer			X									
1.1.c Hire & train veteran speaker with PTSD recovery experience.	Exec.Dir. VA	12 25	12										
1.1.d Identify Reserve/Guard Units & schedule presentations.	Veteran/ Speaker			80									
1.1.e Present information at Guard/Reserve Units.	Veteran/ Speaker				80	80	80	80	80	80	80	80	80

X=In-kind (non-monetary) support

Objective 1.2: Prepare 100 new and experienced volunteers to respond to PTSD-related calls.

Activities	Staff	Jul	Aug	Sep	Oct	Nov	Dec	Jan	Feb	Mar	Apr	May	Jun
1.2.a Develop training materials for volunteers.	VA Writer CP Staff	X 10 10	10 10										
1.2.b Train volunteers for calls about PTSD.	VA Speaker CP Staff		X 20	X 20	X 20								
1.2.c Package training program deliverables for national dissemination.	Writer												20

Goal 2: Identify interest in a public anonymous, confidential 800 hotline for soldiers and their families, and outcomes of an Outreach and Education Campaign.

Objective 2.1: Develop an Interest Survey instrument, disseminate to 3,200 soldiers and their families, and assess likelihood of utilization for a 800 hotline, and what features are vital to the service.

Activities	Staff	Jul	Aug	Sep	Oct	Nov	Dec	Jan	Feb	Mar	Apr	May	Jun
2.1.a Hire, orient & supervise an Evaluation Consultant.	Exec. Director	10	10	1	1	1	1	2	1	1	1	1	2
2.1.b Design Interest Survey.	Evaluator	10	10	1	1	1	1	2	1	1	1	1	2
2.1.c Create protocol for confidential distribution & collection of Survey.	Evaluator			2									
2.1.d Distribute & collect survey from soldiers at visited Units.	Veteran/ Speaker				1	1	1	1	1	1	1	1	1
2.1.e Analyze & report trends in Interest Survey findings.	Evaluator				4	4	4	4	4	4	4	4	4

Objective 2.2: Identify outcomes of the Outreach and Education Campaign.

Activities	Staff	J	A	S	O	N	D	J	F	M	A	M	J
2.2.a Report frequency & results of hotline calls from Soldiers and their families.	Hotline Manager				5	5	5	5	5	5	5	5	5
2.2.b Analyze survey data & information, & hotline logs to develop an outcomes report.	Evaluator				8	8	8	10	8	8	8	10	12

<u>Personnel</u>

Key project staff include: the Executive Director and Hotline Coordinator of CRISIS Pittsburgh; Veteran's Administration experts on PTSD (named earlier); a behavioral health writer and curriculum developer with knowledge of PTSD; a veteran/speaker who has received treatment for PTSD (to be hired); and an evaluation consultant from the Department of Behavioral Health, Graduate School of Public Health, University of Pittsburgh (to be hired).

<u>Sustainability</u>

CRISIS Pittsburgh charges no fees for services, relying instead on support from corporations, foundations, and individual donors. Mr. Rob Conrad has provided a letter of support and is willing to help raise funds to sustain the hotline, and train existing and new volunteers. At least a portion of future volunteers will be recruited from veterans organizations in Western Pennsylvania.

<u>Outcomes and Community Impact</u>

1 . 3,200 soldiers from National Guard and Reserve Units in Western Pennsylvania will receive information about signs of PTSD and the importance of early intervention, which may cause an estimated 1,300 soldiers (40%) to realize they are affected. All soldiers will receive both V.A. and CRISIS Pittsburgh hotline numbers to call for assistance.

2. 100 hotline volunteers will be trained about how to respond to combat-related PTSD. We anticipate a 100% increase in mental health-related calls and requests for support and referrals from soldiers and their families.

3. The Interest Survey and program evaluation will yield data and information about soldiers concerns preventing them from disclosing PTSD, as well as whether they or their families will utilize an anonymous, confidential public 800 hotline for information and support.

CRISIS Pittsburgh will report all findings and financial expenditures to the American Psychiatric Foundation at the end of the grant period. The agency will decide, based upon an analysis of the needs data, whether to establish a nationally accessible 800 hotline. Deliverables will be packaged for national dissemination.

Proposal to the American Psychiatric Foundation
Submitted by CRISIS Pittsburgh

*"Outreach and Education towards a Public 800 Hotline for Early Intervention
of PTSD in Service Combatants Returning from the Middle East"*

Project Budget Summary
Grant Period: July 1, 2006 – June 30, 2007

Revenue:	
American Psychiatric Foundation	$47,000
In-Kind (CRISIS Pittsburgh)	3,000
Total:	**$50,000**
Expenses:	
Personnel Costs	$ 11,214
Professional Fees	17,424
Printing	925
Office Supplies	1,000
Phone/Fax	2,500
Travel	2,700
Meeting Expense	475
Training	6,000
Evaluation	1,500
Other (In-Kind CRISIS Pittsburgh)	3,000
Overhead/Administration	3,262
Total:	**$50,000**

Questions to Consider:

1. *What thoughts came to mind as you read the proposal?*

2. *Can you imagine yourself preparing this type of document for an employer or client?*

3. *What proposals would you like to write for your favored cause or organization?*

How Grants Made a Difference

Here are some examples from my awarded grant projects describing how funding made a difference for various populations and programs:

◊ Home care nurses were trained to respond to depression and anxiety in their homebound patients with Multiple Sclerosis.
◊ "Wounded heroes" received accommodations installed in their homes at no personal cost.
◊ Low-income teens and women who were at risk for complications received pre-natal childbirth services that reduced their incidence of premature births and infant mortality.
◊ An enhanced treatment and lifestyle health program for African-American diabetics was offered at a health care center in a low-income community.
◊ Medical staff visited the homebound elderly to provide health care that prevented ER visits and helped them remain in their homes rather than being placed in long-term care facilities.
◊ Low-income individuals received improved and coordinated care when a community health center integrated onsite mental health care into their system.
◊ High-risk youth received mentoring at school and in the community.
◊ Teen mothers were provided with information and support to bring their newborns and young children to receive immunizations and well-child health visits.
◊ Youth in transition from residential care developed financial literacy skills for emancipation and transition to adulthood.
◊ People with disabilities learned how to become more active participants in the legislative process and voting.
◊ Nonprofit organizations received funding for general operations, marketing outreach, computer servers, facility accessibility and other infrastructure improvements.

What are the Working Conditions for Grant Writers?

Grant writers work in every type and size of organization that is eligible to give and receive grant funding. Examples include: the federal government, state agencies, and local municipalities; Native American tribes; faith-based organizations; community nonprofit and volunteer organizations; academic and medical institutions; and international relief agencies.

Grant writers typically work in an office or home office environment, seated at a computer for lengthy periods of time. The physical working conditions are sedentary. Potential occupational hazards are the same as for office workers in occupations that make use of computers, such as eyestrain, back or neck strain, and overuse of the hands and arms.

There are cycles of giving for every type of funder, with fewer deadlines and funding decisions made during holiday and vacation months. Grant writers may find themselves working overtime when submissions are due. This is not to say that grant writers work every day under the pressure of an imminent deadline. People who write grant proposals on a regular basis learn how to prioritize and plan projects in order to carry out daily tasks in time to effectively meet deadlines.

Organizations sometimes offer greater scheduling flexibility to their employees who serve as proposal writers. Independent contractors who are freelance grant writers and grant consulting businesses often operate from a home office and must establish their own schedules. This level of freedom and flexibility requires daily self-discipline to set up dates, times, and tasks that result in completed projects.

Some grant writers have a different schedule, preferring to start their work later and end their day late in the evening. Still others like to write grant proposals around their children's school schedules.

What type of routine would fit your needs?

☐ Reporting to an established office environment with regular 9 a.m. to 5 p.m. hours of operation.
☐ Working from a home office with a routine and schedule of your own making.

Summary

Grant writing is a form of technical writing that can be both challenging and personally satisfying. All types of organizations and institutions need capable grant professionals. Finding funders and writing proposals that fit the needs of various populations and help to solve problems requires professionals with the interest, knowledge of grants, and writing skills to serve in this valuable role.

TWO

DISCOVERING YOUR CAUSE

People are often too busy to think about the deeper questions concerning how they want to make a difference in the world, or fight for a cause. It may seem like a serious issue to tackle in a book about grants, but people have come to my Grant Career seminars expressing a desire for greater meaningfulness in their occupational choices in middle age, while others have decided to make changes near and after retirement. Many students and graduates prefer to work for a specific cause. You may already be eager to plunge into the grants field, but I urge you to spend some time reflecting on the following questions. Your responses will help to better target your efforts in starting out on this career path.

Your Life Experience

This writing exercise will help to clarify your interests. Imagine yourself taking a walk or having coffee with a trusted friend or mentor—someone who cares enough to ask you...

1. What has been the most meaningful or influential experience of your life?

2. What do you feel is your purpose in life—or what do you care about most passionately?

3. When you read the newspaper or watch the evening news, what social issues and causes do you find most urgent?

4. What are some actions that you would like to take in order to make the world a better place?

Be as specific as possible in your answers. For example, if you are passionate about "ending hunger," are you more concerned with making certain that local families have enough food, or are you interested in ending hunger in developing nations? Stating a specific interest will help you to connect with others who are working on the same issue. You can readily see that finding a solution to stop the violence in your neighborhood may lead you to reach out and work with neighbors, community groups, and leaders.

Can you imagine taking your vision and positive intentions further? Do you want a career change that enables you to make a difference? Let's look at how it may be possible to connect your passion and writing skills to become a grant writer for your cause and community.

Your Writing Skills

The following questions will help you to start exploring whether becoming a grant writer is a good fit with your writing interests, skills and experience. Take a few minutes to find out if past experiences may have prepared you for this career option. There are no wrong answers!

1. *What attracted your interest in the topic of this book?*

2. *To what causes have you contributed time or money?*

3. *Do you have experience as a volunteer or paid writer including samples of your work? Besides writing, what are the other professional skills you can bring to nonprofit organizations?*

4. *Taking into consideration both your personal and professional experiences, what have you written on a regular basis? (Circle all of the items for which you have samples.)*

Press releases	Op-Ed Letters	Journaling	Poetry
Print brochures	Business Plans	Personal essays	Novels
Manuals	Ad copy	Song lyrics	Short stories
Blog	Self-help articles	Science fiction	Screenplays
Websites	Annual reports	Children's picture books	Comedy
Newspaper articles	Research articles	Young adult books	Reflections
Creative non-fiction	Marketing plans	Inspirational articles	Free verse
Fundraising letters	Grant proposals	Memoir / Life Stories	Playwriting

5. *Which medium are you most comfortable using to write?*

   ☐   Pencil & Paper

   ☐   Typewriter

   ☐   Computer

6. *What length document have you written?*

   ☐   Document was a _____ and totaled_____pages.

7. *Approximately what span of time do you feel comfortable writing during an average day?*

   ☐   _____ Hours

8. *List nonprofit organizations at which you have been involved as a:*

   ☐   Volunteer_____

   ☐   Staff or Manager_____

   ☐   Advisor_____

   ☐   Board of Directors_____

9. *Have you written any type of plan or proposal for a business or nonprofit?*

    ☐   Yes

    ☐   No

10. *If you were able to start working for your cause tomorrow, what activities would be listed in your ideal job description?*

Let's look at your responses through the lens of a nonprofit employer searching for an entry-level grant writer. People enter employment in the nonprofit sector with various personal and professional qualifications. It is important to have a desire to write coupled with strong English writing skills. A college degree in Journalism, Communications or English is not always required. Many employers will consider equivalent writing experience and writing samples. Some agencies do not require experience with grants and instead look to hire and develop people from within the organization.

Question 1: *What attracted your attention to the topic of this book?*

If you were to mention in an interview that you became interested in applying after you read this book, a sharp interviewer might ask what you found most interesting. Maybe the safest answer would be "all of it." We will discuss grant salaries later, but nonprofits are looking for employees who are motivated by their cause as much or more than money.

Question 2: *To what causes have you given time or money?*

Is there a clear connection between your interests and choices made to support your cause with donations of your time and money? Potential employers will pay attention to not only what you say about being committed to nonprofit work, but the facts reflected in your volunteer experiences.

Question 3: *Do you have experience as a volunteer or paid writer including samples of your work? Besides writing, what are the other professional skills you can bring to nonprofit organizations?*

Applicants for grant positions are routinely required to provide proof of their capabilities in the form of writing samples. Some of the other skills and experience compatible with an entry-level grants position include: management and administration; technical writing and communications; public relations and marketing; and fundraising.

Question 4: *Taking into consideration both your personal and professional experiences, what have you written on a regular basis?*

In the absence of sample grants, the next best samples to sell your skills are listed in the two left-hand columns. These are examples of professional, technical and non-fiction writing as opposed to the creative writing genres shown in the right-hand columns. You may want to reconsider this career choice if you are only interested in creative writing and your goal is to create a book of poetry or the next great American novel.

Question 5: *Which medium are you most comfortable using to write?*

Writing grant proposals involves using word processing and spreadsheet software, so you must have comfort with computer technology and speedy keyboard skills.

Question 6-7: *What length document have you written? Approximately what span of time do you feel comfortable writing during an average day?*

You might be surprised to know that some grant proposals are very short at just a few pages, so the length of documents you are accustomed to writing is not necessarily a barrier at entry-level. The length of time that you are able to write, and the length of the documents that you prepare, will increase significantly as you practice and gain experience with writing grant proposals.

Question 8: *List nonprofit organizations at which you have been involved as a volunteer, staff member, director, advisor, or board of directors.*

Nonprofit employers pay attention to not only what you say about being committed to their cause and nonprofit work, but these should be reflected in specific items in your resume.

Question 9: *Have you written any type of plan or proposal for a business or non-profit organization?*

A familiarity with business plans can be helpful, but there are also specialized training programs that teach the technical knowledge, terminology, and skills used in writing grant proposals.

Question 10: *If you were able to start working for your cause tomorrow, what activities would be listed in your ideal job description?*

This is a classic interview question. There will be more information about the grant writer's role and responsibilities in the next two chapters. You may want to come back to this question later to find out how well your ideal job description fits with grant related duties. If you are passionate about making a difference, and are willing to learn and practice proposal writing skills, these qualities can help you to succeed.

Considering Multiple Causes

It is worth mentioning that successful grant professionals understand how to handle projects for multiple causes and organizations. If you feel undecided or wish to consider the full range of possibilities, use this exercise to identify your interests according to various program areas that receive grants.

Rate Your Interests (Check all that apply.)

Program Areas	Low 1	2	3	4	High 5
Advocacy					
Aging & Cross-Generational					
Agriculture & Farming					
Animals					
Arts & Humanities					
Community & Economic Development					
Conservation / Ecology					
Disaster Relief, Emergency Services					
Disease Prevention & Health Promotion					
Education (Pre-K to 12th Grade)					
Employment, Job Training, Workforce					
Environment					
Faith-based / Religious					
Family & Youth Development					
Food, Nutrition & Hunger					
Healthcare					
Higher Education					
Historic Preservation					
Housing & Homelessness					
Immigration					
International Affairs & Relief					
Literacy					
Medical Research					
Mental Health, Trauma, Substance Abuse					
Poverty					
Technology, STEM Learning					
Violence, Assault & Abuse					

Count up your check marks. Looking at the whole chart, which areas are highly rated? What patterns do you see?

Chances are good that there are nonprofit organizations in your community or region that match your interests. Be assured that you do not have to specialize in one cause in order to become successful! Many grant professionals handle projects for all types of nonprofit organizations, near and far, and every interest under the sun!

The benefits of *not* limiting your writing to a single cause:

- You might learn faster by practicing and gaining experience with a variety of projects.

- You may be able to pinpoint interests later or discover a cause as your career evolves.

- If your passion is spread among a group of causes, there may be more projects available as a freelancer for several organizations.

Consider this question carefully:

If working for a cause is not your primary source of inspiration, what will motivate you to work hard in this career?

Grant Writing for My Cause

I loved writing and kept journals from an early age. My passion was divided between creative and athletic activities including writing stories on women's sports for my high school and college newspapers. One of my favorite graduate school courses was Grant Writing and Fundraising. This exposure to the nonprofit sector drew me into working as a manager of nonprofit health and fitness programs. I enjoyed developing marketing plans and writing brochures.

In my mid-forties, I decided to pursue a professional writing career and was hired as a technical writer to develop publications for a psychology consulting firm. When the company moved out of town, I saw an opportunity to try grant writing. I wrote my first grant proposal as a volunteer, and when it was funded, continued working with the agency as a freelancer.

One of the great benefits of starting a business has been the flexibility to use my writing skills for grant proposals and other writing for my cause. I have written a blog, and published articles and a book on wellness. I wrote the book you are holding between grant projects.

Grant writing is a meaningful and financially rewarding use of my writing skills. I've helped nonprofits to earn millions of dollars for new and much needed projects. And there have been many instances when my health knowledge provided an extra edge in developing new programs that won grants. My story is an example of how people enter the grants profession. This work has offered me an opportunity to use writing skills to make a difference for a wide range of populations, causes, and social interests.

I agree with the leading grant author Dr. Beverly Browning when she states in *Grant Writing for Dummies* that: "...pursuing grants is one of the most interesting occupations in the world."

Summary

Simply put, "your cause" is the difference that you want to make for society (the public good) and believe in deeply enough to commit your time and energy for long-term change.

Nonprofit organizations welcome people with transferable skills from previous employment, especially if you share a passion for their work as reflected in your volunteer and writing experiences.

Working as a grant proposal writer, whether for one cause or a broad range of interests, is a way to focus your life's purpose and participate in the work of organizations that are creating a better world.

THREE

MAKING MEANING AND MONEY AS A GRANT PROFESSIONAL

Career Opportunities

Imagine the responses if you asked people on the street or at nearly any office, "Who likes to write grant proposals?" Once they leave high school or college, many people dislike writing in general and recoil from complex writing projects. As a result, organizations are willing to pay employees and independent contractors for the specialized services of grant writing. Following are some of the employment options.

The grant writer can be a volunteer, advisor, or board member who gives their personal time and efforts without an expectation of payment to advance work in a favored cause, organization, or community.

A grant writer can be any part-time or full-time paid employee whose job description includes responsibility for the agency's grant submissions, including grant research, writing, reporting, and administration.

At smaller nonprofits, the executive director often has the responsibility of writing grant proposals, along with other management and fundraising duties.

Mid-size organizations may assign employees to dual roles in fundraising and grant writing. Titles include development director, development associate, development assistant, fundraiser, and grant writer. There is often an expectation that staff with general fundraising responsibilities will develop grant writing skills along with carrying out other duties, such as meeting with prospective donors, writing copy for a newsletter or website, maintaining a donor database, organizing and marketing special events, helping with mailings and phone calls, and working with volunteers.

Large nonprofit organizations and institutions may employ a grant writer, grant manager, grant coordinator, or grant administrator to research, write, manage and report on a continuous flow of proposals. Others may hire a development writer to prepare grant proposals along with writing annual reports, newsletters, and feature articles for the agency. The foundation relations manager is a relatively new position that combines grant writing and responsibility for building and maintaining relationships with funders.

A research grant writer may be a subject matter expert with an advanced degree and in-depth technical knowledge, including proficiency in project planning, administration, and proposal writing. For example, medical research companies, hospital systems, and academic institutions hire doctoral level experts with titles such as project manager or project investigator that combines grant writing skills with knowledge of the language and research processes of their specialty.

Large institutions may hire a director of advancement based on their business experience and ability to collaborate in writing grant proposals for major projects.

Subject matter experts and experienced grant professionals may submit their credentials to be a grant reviewer who is paid to objectively evaluate and rate complex grant proposals for government agencies and foundations.

Individuals with knowledge and experience in both nonprofit programs and financial management may be hired in grant making organizations as a foundation program officer, foundation director, grant writer, or grant administrator.

An individual can act as a self-employed independent grant writing contractor, freelance grant writer, or sub-contractor with the opportunity to negotiate contractual relationships for themselves. This business entity is a "sole proprietor" who contracts with organizations to provide grant services on a temporary or casual basis.

Grant consultant is a title used by more experienced grant professionals with small business, which may provide services locally and nationally, and often advertise through a website and social media. Some grant consultants also offer other writing and services such as for books, manuals, business plans, business communications, speeches, advertising, public relations, fundraising copy writing, and applications for nonprofit status.

Fundraising consultants often have several years of advanced training and nonprofit fundraising experience, and offer grant writing as one of several services related to planning and carrying out fundraising campaigns. It should be noted that many states require a special license to offer independent grant and/or fundraising services. Each state has different rules and regulations for independent contractors in this field. One of the major differences is that fundraisers often initiate requests for funding from individual donors. In contrast, grant consultants often respond to current open grant opportunities and Requests for Proposals (RFP) from foundations, corporate sponsors and government entities. They may help build relationships with grant makers.

Sometimes grant professionals describe the focus of our work in terms like "generalist" or "specialist" based upon whether we work on proposals in every field of interest or specific content areas. Grant professionals may also specialize in providing specific services, such as funder research, evaluation, or training.

Individuals with entrepreneurial vision and leadership skills may find unique opportunities to serve their chosen cause by becoming the founder of a new nonprofit organization or for-profit company. In this case, business planning, project development and proposal writing skills are useful in addition to knowing how to start and manage an organization.

Defining Success

Like other professionals, we describe our work in terms of satisfaction and financial rewards. Grant writers and nonprofit organizations determine success in a variety of ways. I have measured my performance by meeting or exceeding grant funding goals. Other measures of success include:

- Achieving agency's annual goal amount for grants.

- Increased number and amount of grants awarded over a period of time.

- Size of grant awards and notoriety of grant funders.

- Grant projects recognized as groundbreaking, innovative, or meeting a significant need.

- Success Rate: the percentage of grant proposals submitted compared to grants awarded (e.g., ten proposals submitted and eight grants awarded equals a success rate of 80 percent).

- Return on Investment (ROI): the overall cost of producing one or more grant proposals in proportion to the grant amounts awarded (e.g., if a government grant proposal costs $5,000 to write through staff and contractor efforts and the grant awarded is $100,000, the agency's ROI is 20:1 or a return of $20 for every $1 spent in development).

In the World of Grants, the bottom line measure of success is being able to consistently write grants that receive funding.

Once you've landed a staff position or client, you will need to prove that you are capable of doing the job. You and the organization will not be satisfied over time with a low rate of success. In business, the new sales person must learn how to convert prospects into paying customers. With study, practice, and experience, you can learn how to make proposals highly appealing to funders.

Meaning and Motivation

The everyday work of preparing grant proposals involves challenges, especially the focused thinking and writing for sometimes long periods of time. The questions in Chapter Two were designed to connect you with the deep-seated, positive passion for your chosen cause, which can offer emotional inspiration and motivation needed to work through demanding days.

Realizing the Meaningful Aspects of Grants

Feeling a sense of purpose and appreciating what a grant award will mean to the organization and the people it serves always gives me the lift and drive to push through long hours of writing. In my experience, lengthy and complex proposals have had what I affectionately refer to as the "tired out stage" that occurs when the excitement of starting it is past, fascination with the subject matter has worn thin, and I'm nearing completion, but not quite done.

The final phase of writing a complex proposal involves checking detailed information, revising drafts, editing and repeating this process with staff and management input until the proposal is satisfactory. Over the years I've become efficient and able to cut through the mental fatigue involved in preparing lengthy documents. It is always a thrill to finish and submit the grant application on deadline! When my first grant proposal received funding, I was not expecting the satisfaction and sense of accomplishment at using my writing skills to raise money for services with a tangible impact on people's lives. It felt like the ultimate reward.

I believe it's important to be aware of personal motivation and the balance between making meaning and money. If the "meaning" side of the equation is present, you will be able to tap into your passion, connect with others who share your cause, and find the mental stamina for challenging projects. We should expect fair and reasonable compensation for our hard work and rates based on a track record of grant success. However, if you expect to "get rich quick" as a novice grant writer, that self-serving motivation may be unrealistic and unwelcome at many nonprofit organizations.

Making Money

The question, "How much can I make as a grant proposal writer?" can be difficult to answer. Estimating salaries is not an exact science. Yet, this is rightfully among the first questions people looking to enter any new career field want answered *before* they expend their valuable time and effort.

Here are some of the factors to consider in projecting potential salary and growth as an employed grant writer at a community-based nonprofit organization.

- Hourly rates and employee salaries will be higher in geographic areas where the cost of living is higher, especially coastal and major metropolitan areas. The range of salaries and fees that the market will bear is lower in the South, Midwest and in small towns and rural areas.

- Salary levels will be lower at smaller nonprofit organizations.

- Overall interest and demand for grant professionals will be higher in state capital cities and regions with a large concentration of nonprofit agencies, institutions of higher learning, governmental agencies and grant making organizations.

- A basic level of grant training, writing skill, and experience will often be expected. A college writing degree may not be enough to be hired at large organizations. A resume with professional experience and training, along with writing samples and awarded grants list may be requested as proof of competency.

- An interest in grant writing, along with work experience and skill in related fields may lead to a higher paying position combining grants with management, finance, programming, marketing or fundraising.

Potential income as a freelancer, consultant, and small business owner depends on the factors stated above and other issues.

- Strength of the economy, charitable giving, and interest in the cause(s) related to your grant writing experience.

- Number of local consultants and nonprofits that provide technical assistance with grants that will be in competition for projects.

- A strong network of professional colleagues, agency contacts, other personal referral sources, and marketing efforts that helps build and maintain a "pipeline" and steady flow of projects.

- The number of years providing services and having an established business reputation.

While salary studies have been conducted by the Grant Professionals Association, there are no national pay standards or a union scale. The competency continuum and salary ranges shown on the following chart for grant professionals were drawn from web research, information collected at interviews, posted job descriptions, salary reports from various nonprofit and professional sources, and government bulletins.

Competency Continuum		
ENTRY-LEVEL	**INTERMEDIATE**	**ADVANCED/EXPERT**
Letters of Inquiry & Short Proposals Family Foundations	**Foundation and Corporate Grants United Way Applications Local/State/Federal Government**	**Federal Government Large National & International Foundations**
Sample Income Range		
	Hourly Fees	
$15 - $25 per hour	$30 - $60 - $80 per hour	$90 - $200 per hour
	Project Fees	
$1,500 per project Example: Research funders and prepare 5 LOI or short proposals	$3,500 per project Example: Research funders and prepare five full proposals	$5,000+ per project Example: Research funders and prepare five full proposals
$2,000-$3,000 Sub-Contractor for a government application (40-100 hours)	$4,000-$8,000 One local/state or federal government application (40– 100+ hours)	$8,000-$10,000+ One federal government or international application (80-100+ hours)
	Full-Time Salaries	
$30,000-$45,000/year + Benefits	$45,000-$70,000/year + Benefits	$70,000–$100,000+/year + Benefits

Hourly and project fees are charged by independent grant contractors who set their own terms and rates. Salary ranges are for full-time employment as a grant proposal writer for nonprofit organizations. Expert grant professionals can make a higher income as an independent contractor, while salaried employment can carry exceptional benefits. Find your possible local wages at http://www.salaries.com + "free salary wizard" + "grants/proposal writer" + your zip code (this site compiles data from both nonprofit and corporate proposal writer positions).

There is an ongoing debate about the benefits, risks and ethics of different compensation practices (salaried, fee-based, and contingency). Contingency payment (when grant writers accept payment for services in the form of a percentage of the grant and only if the grant is awarded) is widely viewed as unethical and unprofessional by leading national grant and fundraising associations. The grant preparer's salary or fee is usually paid from the agency's administrative overhead, like accounting or other professional fees. While contingency payments are made to sales professionals in the corporate sector, and I was tempted in my start-up years to accept it rather than lose a contract, it is honestly an "under the table" arrangement because funders will not award a grant if they know upfront that a portion of their grant is paying for proposal writing instead of the proposed purpose. Information on ethical guidelines is available to GPA members at http://www.grantprofessionals.org.

Job Growth Outlook

Several factors are contributing to growth in grant writing as a specialized profession (and distinct from technical and copy writing for the corporate sector.) The nonprofit sector has been growing faster than the rest of the economy. Opportunities to write grant proposals are expected to increase as Grant Writer and Grant Consultant have emerged as distinct occupations. The U.S. Department of Labor, Bureau of Labor Statistics has published an informative article about the work carried out by grant writers.[3] Whether you are considering employment in a salaried position within an organization, part-time freelance grant writer, or launching a grant consulting company, the major duties involve researching funders and writing grant proposals for grant seekers or grant makers.

Remember that grant writers may also be called upon to perform broader duties. At nonprofit organizations, you may also serve as the "in-house writing expert." You may write and edit all outgoing fundraising correspondence, public relations materials, annual reports and brochures, or manuals, and even website content. You may be called upon to serve as both a grant writer and fundraiser, or a grants manager. Thus, the functional role and job title of "Grant Writer" is currently associated with the following other U.S. Department of Labor occupational classifications.

---

3   http://www.bls.gov/careeroutlook/2014/youre-a-what/grant-writer (September 2014).

	Median Pay (May 2015)		Job Outlook (2014-2024)
	Per Year	Per Hour	
Writers and Authors	$60,250	$28.97	2%
Technical Writers	$70,240	$33.77	10%
Public Relations Specialists	$56,770	$27.29	1%
Fundraisers	$52,970	$25.47	2%
Social and Community Service Managers	$63,530	$30.54	1%

Source: Bureau of Labor Statistics, U.S. Department of Labor, *Occupational Outlook Handbook*, 2015.

Grant Writing as an Encore Career

Individuals who have retired and are considering grant writing as a rewarding second career or freelancing opportunity may realize the reported benefits of working during the retirement years. Working one year increases annual retirement income about nine percent and working five years boosts income about fifty-six percent, with a higher impact on lower income individuals. Many older workers are self-employed and self-employment rates increase with age. Part-time and part-year work is common at older ages and working longer may also contribute positively to health and mental health, according to the Retirement Policy Center at the Urban Institute.

Questions to Consider:

1. *What does professional success mean to you – can you list the goals for your career and stage of life?*

2. *From what you have learned thus far, in what ways could grant writing offer the meaning and money that you are seeking in a career or business opportunity?*

Summary

There are many opportunities for career growth and development in the World of Grants that include writing, researching, consulting, management, teaching, and business. Such growth depends upon the grant proposal writer's ability to consistently and successfully obtain grant awards. People who want a career in which they can use their writing ability to produce positive benefits for their cause and community can experience personal satisfaction (make meaning) and receive good compensation (make money) for their efforts.

FOUR

BECOMING SUCCESSFUL
IN THE GRANTS PROFESSION

Personal Attributes

At this point, one of your questions might be, "do I have the attributes or ability to become a grant writer?" The purpose of the following activity is to raise your awareness of characteristics that you may have in common with grant professionals. The term "attributes" is used here as a general descriptor for "temperament, personality, strengths, and other characteristics of self." This is an informal inventory. Various descriptors were gathered from discussions with colleagues and clients, and traits requested in job postings.

Exercise: Circle your 10 best personal and work-related attributes.

focused	multi-tasker	persuasive	logical	articulate
productive	dependable	tech-savvy	flexible	team player
persistent	enthusiastic	organized	inquisitive	detail-oriented
sociable	attentive	knowing	unique	generous
sensitive	bright	bookish	perfectionist	imaginative
thoughtful	thrifty	courteous	creative	compassionate
trustworthy	objective	independent	personable	competitive
optimistic	accountable	adaptable	promotional	decisive
passionate	strategic	informed	skillful	entrepreneurial

Interpretation:

The top three lines list traits found in job postings for grant proposal writers.

The bottom three lines show attributes of independent grant contractors who write and consult with organizations, and have additional responsibilities of managing and marketing a small business.

Question to Consider:

Which of your personal and professional attributes do you have in common with grant writers and self-employed grant contractors?

The purpose of this inventory is to help raise your awareness of attributes you may have in common with grant professionals; it cannot predict success. Some aspects of human beings are unchanging, and people with various personalities and temperaments are successful in the grants profession. You can enhance the attributes associated with a grant career and business by building on your natural strengths with suggestions described in this chapter.

Knowledge and Skill Requirements

When hiring a grant writer, employers advertise for candidates with one or both of these qualifications:

- A strong background in writing, in the form of a college degree in English, Communications, Journalism, or Professional Writing plus experience.

- Relevant combination of experience with grants as demonstrated through a resume, grant training, writing samples, references, and a list of awarded grants.

Even when an employer advertises for the first set of qualifications, I have frequently succeeded in making a case for hiring me with the second set. In nearly every instance the candidate with proven grant writing capabilities wins the position over an individual with a general writing degree who is lacking grants experience. For entry-level grant positions, agencies also may hire individuals with a strong interest in their cause, writing aptitude as demonstrated by a writing sample, and willingness to attend grant training workshops. Larger institutions look for advanced grant competencies, management experience, verified success in winning grant awards, and national certification.

Next, you can see an actual job description for an entry-level grant writer at a mid-size nonprofit organization. The salary range was $30,000 to $43,000 with benefits (annual two-week paid vacation and five sick days; medical, dental, disability and life insurance; and 403B Retirement Plan).

JOB DESCRIPTION: GRANT WRITER

Primary Function

Responsible for writing proposals and researching public and private foundation sources for both unrestricted operating revenue and restricted projects and for submission of accurate reports for grant funded projects.

Duties and Responsibilities

1. Researches grant opportunities from various sources that match the goals of the agency.

2. Gathers information from staff and coordinates/writes grant proposals.

3. Works with the Development Director to develop/manage effective working relationships with grantors and facilitate approval of grants.

4. Follows up with grantors to determine/monitor the status of grant applications.

5. Works with Fiscal Manager to gather financial information necessary to submit proposal budgets and grant reports.

6. Provides monthly reports on the status of grant proposals.

7. Supports agency fund raising and public relations activities to create a positive image of the agency and a public climate conducive to financial support.

8. Adheres to ethical practices and confidentiality in communication with donors, staff, clients and others. Adheres to Donor Bill of Rights.

9. Reports to: Development Director

Minimum Qualifications

- Bachelor's Degree in Communications or a related field, or equivalent experience

- Ability to locate grant-related and funder information on the Internet

- Knowledge of formats, definitions and language of grant proposals

- Broad understanding of the organization's programs

- One to three years experience in grant writing preferred

- Strong written communication skills with a demonstrated ability to write clear, structured, articulate, and persuasive proposals

- Strong editing skills

- Ability to work independently to meet deadlines

Learning Curve for Developing Grant Proposal Writing Competency

The World of Grants is a competitive environment in which grant proposal writers are expected to continually learn, proactively monitor and research grant opportunities, cultivate relationships with funders, and submit proposals for funding. Career advancement depends on sustaining the motivation and output for securing grants. If the grant writer's job sounds daunting, you should know that many people have taught themselves how to write grant proposals by trial and error in the course of their employment. However, there are plenty of informational and training resources available today and this section describes an effective approach to learning. You can develop grant competency by steering your way through the learning curve involving grant training, developing skills through supervised practice, and gaining experience with various proposal formats used by funders.

This chart depicts the general perceived level of effort in the early, middle and later stages of learning how to prepare proposals for various types of support and funders.

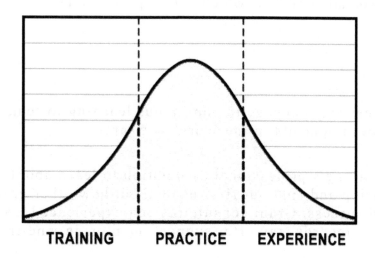

TRAINING   PRACTICE   EXPERIENCE

Learning Effort for Grant Competency

Grant Training

The volume of information involved in learning all aspects of grant seeking and proposal writing will feel overwhelming, like an "uphill journey" at first. Attending online and in person workshops is a popular way to get started.

There are many different types of training opportunities available and a variety of providers. The methods of learning include webinar presentations, workshops, and on-the-job training. Reputable professional development and training organizations provide group seminars, webinars and online courses. Providers include community colleges, universities, nonprofit organizations, libraries, grant companies, and national associations. In most instances, a certificate of attendance is earned. The length of workshops typically ranges from one to five days. Briefer training events are often presented in a lecture-discussion format, while lengthier courses tend to incorporate individual or team proposal writing practice. There is no single book, online course, or workshop that teaches everything one needs to know about successful grant writing.

Certification is not required to be hired as an entry-level grant writer; however, it is worthwhile to pursue credentialing because it helps to verify qualifications to employers and clients. The Grant Professionals Certification Institute (GPCI) has established a list of competencies that verify the attainment of grant knowledge, skills and experience. Grant professionals demonstrate their capabilities by proving a minimum number of awarded grants over a period of years and satisfying other criteria in order to become eligible for the examination. GPCI is affiliated with the Grant Professionals Association (GPA), which offers professional development webinars and conferences.

Tips

1. Grant professionals engage in continuous learning to remain informed of the latest developments in the World of Grants.

2. Consider joining a professional association to learn about the field of grantsmanship and find out first-hand about how other grant writers have found success. Grant consultants and experienced trainers with proven track records may offer support, mentoring, and trial projects.

3. Start out developing your knowledge and skills at affordable local workshops. See the Resources section for more information about the various training and professional development programs available from reputable organizations.

4. Seek out local nonprofit meetings and forums. These events allow beginners to learn about the organizations and projects that need grants.

Supervised Practice

After learning the basics about grants, supervised proposal writing practice helps novice grant writers to advance in the field. In his book *Outliers*, Malcolm Gladwell popularized the theory that it takes 10,000 hours of deliberate practice to reach the level of mastery associated with expert performance in every endeavor from athletics to business, and the arts, which includes writing.

Does the "10,000-Hour Rule" apply to grant writing? Grant proposal writers who diligently write four hours each day during the work week for fifty weeks per year will reach the mark in ten years. In my experience, it took three to five years of well-rounded proposal writing practice along with feedback to develop enough skill to produce grant applications at a consistently high success rate. Learning the complexities of proposal writing may result in mastery only if the doer is practicing the right skills in the first place. (Imagine learning to play the violin without the feedback of a music teacher!) You could spend hundreds of hours writing proposals that go unfunded unless you receive feedback before submission in order to correct obvious errors.

Tips

1. Find a grant writing mentor or proposal coach. You may be employed in a grant position and reach a professional level of competency much sooner than the 10,000-hour benchmark.

2. Look for a supervisor, mentor, or coach with grant writing experience who has the time and willingness to offer quality feedback on your proposals.

3. Feedback is only as valuable as the person who is delivering it. Look for a supervisor who has demonstrated their mastery of grant seeking with grant awards from all types of funders (foundations, corporations, United Way, Government) over the course of their careers.

4. A proposal coach delivers constructive pointers in a positive manner. The mentoring process should result in an increase in know-how about writing different types of proposals, build writing skills, and enable you to improve the quality and quantity of grant applications. In addition, practicing the right skills and attaining grant awards will build confidence.

5. Some experienced grant consultants offer internships, apprenticeships, or private training and proposal coaching that assists novice grant writers to learn quickly and get on-track in this career.

Gaining Experience

Grant writers who have arrived at this phase of the learning curve are capable of taking on larger, complex proposals and projects involving multiple funders. It takes broad-based experience over a period of time to learn how to consistently win grant awards of any amount, requiring any format, from any type of funder. Grant professionals with years of know-how, experience, and success have developed effective systems and greater efficiency that enables them to expend much less time and effort in assessing agency readiness and needs, planning projects, researching funders and writing proposals. In a word, the learning curve and work seems "easier."

Tips

1. Set up a simple log or spreadsheet to track your grant proposal submissions and awards with information such as:

   ☐ Agency name

   ☐ Proposal title

   ☐ Brief description of your role and number of hours worked on the project

   ☐ Submission date, funder, and amount

   ☐ Award amount and year, or reason for failure

2. Make a goal to attend advanced training and work on projects with larger awards for each type of grant maker:

   ☐ Corporate sponsors and foundations

   ☐ Public, private, and community foundations

   ☐ United Way

   ☐ Local, state, and federal governments

3. Be continuously ready to respond to new grant opportunities. Develop a monitoring system to receive email alerts from funders. Observe happenings and trends in the grants field through news channels and social media. Grant professionals must be interested in learning every day— we are called upon to be proactive in positioning agencies to apply for grants. Pay attention to:

   ☐ Agency strategic, business and program plans

   ☐ National and federal evidence-based programs and promising practices

   ☐ Agency evaluations and outcomes for the programs and populations served

   ☐ Grant announcements from funders

   ☐ News about nonprofit partners, collaborative ventures and competitors

   ☐ Societal and economic problems that have an impact on charitable giving

Avoiding Grant Schemes and Scams

Due to the growing awareness of grants, and grant career and business opportunities, there is a great deal of confusing advertising on the Internet. Various "get rich quick" ads are either business schemes (misleading but not illegal) or outright scams.

In general, you should know that advertisement for "free grants" and "free government grants" is a deceptive marketing practice. Only about one percent of grants are given to individuals. It is technically true that individuals can be eligible, but the public is rarely eligible to receive a "free grant" from online sources. The definition of a grant (money given for public benefit) actually means that individuals are not permitted to personally profit from grants. Most grants are given to nonprofits that provide programs and services, and this is the designated route wherein individuals receive the benefit of grant monies. Remember that grants are not actually free money with no strings attached. An application or grant proposal and reporting is required.

Inside a Grant Scam

A surprising number of web-based businesses employ advertising schemes and outright scams to make money on the public's interest in grants. Out of curiosity about how a grant scheme works, I responded to a telemarketing call to receive a Free Grant CD that promised to give any member of the public an opportunity to win grants. The CD was to contain a list of available grants and instructions in how to apply. I had to give a credit card number to pay for shipping the CD to my home. The CD arrived in 10 days with a list of government agencies (available on federal government websites at no cost). Although it was promised in the pitch and table of contents, there was no information about how to apply for grants. I knew that accepting this offer was risky, so I gave a credit card for an account containing a small amount of money that I had planned to close. Sure enough, the company attempted to charge my account the next month for an unauthorized subscription to future CDs. In conducting further research on the company, I found an elaborate companion website set up to give "objective" reports on grant businesses for the purpose of legitimizing the scam company. Tracing the company's name led me to an owner who had started more than 1000 other Internet-based companies.

Protect yourself from schemes and scams when purchasing grant training products and services.

- ☐ Evaluate whether the offering is a good investment for your career. Advanced technical topics may not be helpful or understandable for your first grant training experience.

- ☐ Ask other grant writers or a mentor about their experiences with the trainer and organization.

- ☐ Ask questions about the instructor's background such as their credentials and years of experience, grant success, affiliations, and years of instructional experience.

When in doubt, check the Better Business Bureau for complaints at http://www.bbb.org. Report grant scams to the Federal Trade Commission at https://www.ftccomplaintassistant.gov.

Ethical Grantsmanship

Grant professionals face ethical issues and must exercise good judgment about confidentiality, financial, and other aspects of grant seeking and proposal writing. It is important to become familiar with standards of practice in order to strengthen your possibilities of success and also avoid illegal, detrimental, and poorly informed grant practices.

One of the best explanations of sound practices can be found in *Grantsmanship: Program Planning and Proposal Writing* by Norton J. Kiritz, Founder of The Grantsmanship Center, Inc. (TGCI).[8]

Summary

Grant proposal writers become successful in this profession by: (1) developing positive attributes and strengths; (2) navigating a learning curve of grant training, practice, and experience to develop competency; and (3) upholding standards of ethical grantsmanship.

---

[8] *Grantsmanship: Progam Planning & Proposal Writing*, by Norton J. Kiritz, Updated & Expanded by Barbara Floersch, Edited by Cathleen E. Kiritz, Published by The Grantsmanship Center (1974-2014). Available for purchase at www.tgci.com.

FIVE

GRANT CAREER ACTION PLAN

I hope you have enjoyed learning about the World of Grants. Remember how we started out with just one goal in mind? My purpose has been to offer you the information needed to explore this career option. You've been reading and answering questions about whether the grant career path might be a good "fit" for you. Let's see whether this book has helped you to arrive at a clear answer. Please be honest with yourself, because after all, this is your life and career!

Decision Point: Is grant writing your next career?

☐ Yes   ☐ Maybe   ☐ No

If you answered "Yes," continue with The Grant Career Action Plan, a chapter that will guide you through ten steps for getting hired (and re-hired) for grant positions and projects.

If you answered "Maybe," perhaps you are uncertain about grant proposal writing as your next career move. Remember this is also a valuable secondary skill-set that may enhance your chances of being hired for other positions. You may find some of the following steps to be helpful in "trying out" proposal writing, or to get ready for other positions or projects. Consider attending local nonprofit conferences, and look for chapter meetings of the Grant Professionals Association (GPA) or Association of Fundraising Professionals (AFP) where you can become involved with nonprofits and discover your niche. (See "General Nonprofit Careers" and "General Fundraising" in the Resources section.)

If you answered "No," congratulations on arriving at an honest answer! If grant writing is not a good fit you may want to consider serving in a different capacity for your community. Volunteer for board service or fundraising events, or donate goods, services, time, and money to an organization that needs your help and passion.

Getting Ready to Take Action

I have often been approached via email and in person by aspiring grant writers wanting specific information about how to get hired. I developed a Grant Career Seminar and this chapter to provide my best advice in the form of a structured action plan. Each step has been invaluable to me in getting hired and re-hired for grant positions and projects.

Keep in mind that taking action on a new career involves both effort and risk. This chapter offers an approach based upon my personal and professional experiences. Just like any other career book you read or seminar you might attend to learn about a new opportunity, following through on the activities described here will be entirely your responsibility and at your discretion.

Grant Career Action Plan: 10 Steps to Hire

Starting a new career can be complicated and sometimes overwhelming, so I encourage you to take it (literally) one step at a time. The Grant Career Action Plan offers a step-by-step approach with information and suggested activities that are generally self-guided and low cost, requiring little or no previous experience to get started. You may be able to skip steps or rearrange the order based upon your past work experience. There are no hard and fast rules or time frames. Feel free to adapt the information to your unique situation. Steps 1 to 4 consist of activities for getting ready to enter a grant career. Steps 5 to 8 provide suggestions about grant training and mentoring leading to completion of your first grant proposal. Steps 9 and 10 offer job entry advice to help you perform well in interviews and get hired.

Each step is composed of:

A. Rationale: Reason why the step is recommended

B. Career-Builders: Information and activities to assist you in getting started

C. Completion Standard: A way to know when you're ready to move ahead to the next step

Grant Career Action Plan Checklist

	10 Steps to Hire:	✓
Career Readiness	1. Brush-Up Your Writing Skills	____
	2. Assess Your Lifestyle	____
	3. Organize a Home Office	____
	4. Build a Network in Your Community	____
Career Training	5. Learn about Grant Seeking and Proposal Writing	____
	6. Find a Mentor and Write a Grant Proposal	____
	7. Join a Group for Grant Professionals	____
	8. Develop a Resume and Portfolio for Grants	____
Job Entry	9. Cultivate Grant Jobs	____
	10. Sell Your Grant-Related Skills at Interviews to Get Hired (and Re-Hired)	____

Step 1: Brush-Up Your Writing Skills

Rationale

This step is for people who are concerned about their writing skills or want suggestions about how to improve their writing style.

Career-Builders

If you know an experienced grant professional, by all means ask that person for feedback on a writing sample such as the assignment below.

This assignment comes from a real life situation. Early in my grant career, I interviewed for a grant writing contractor position. My writing sample won me the job. This is a great warm-up activity for job seeking.

Letter Writing Assignment

I am an employer who has interviewed you for an entry-level grant position. I enjoyed talking with you, but I am having difficulty choosing between you and another well-qualified candidate. To gain more insight into your writing abilities, I ask both of you for overnight writing samples. Please provide me with a one-page business letter that makes the best case for why I should hire you as a grant writer for my agency. You should especially emphasize the skills and experience you will bring to our agency's mission.

Hint: Make up an ideal scenario with your favorite cause and an organization where you would like to be hired. Use what you've learned about employer expectations and make your "best case" for hiring you.

Next, view the sample employment letter that won me the contractor position at www.grantepreneur.com.

Completion Standard

☐ You have received feedback on your writing assignment.

☐ You have polished your writing skills using the writing topics, tips and tools at http://www.grantepreneur.com.

Step 2: Assess Your Lifestyle

Rationale

Job changes sometimes call for modifying one's lifestyle. Getting started in a grant career may involve adjustments of your personal, family, or household habits, as well as assessing your financial situation in order to make a decision about your entry-level employment.

Career-Builders

For each item below, circle the answer (under choice A or B) that is most true for you.

Lifestyle Assessment

Lifestyle Assessment:	Choice A	Choice B
1. Physical activity is …	___ a regular habit	___ not in my weekly routine
2. My health is …	___ excellent or good	___ average or poor
3. In stressful situations I …	___ try to relax or take a break	___ eat, drink, smoke or snap
4. Hours of seated work …	___ is reasonably comfortable	___ hurts or makes me restless
5. Using a computer is …	___ frequent and easy	___ infrequent and difficult
6. In this career change …	___ family and friends are supportive	___ family and friends don't know or support me yet
7. My family and I …	___ talk and plan together	___ communicate with difficulty
8. My personal obligations …	___ allow scheduling flexibility	___ cannot be adjusted for deadlines
9. I must have work that …	___ permits independence	___ is traditional and "low risk"
10. My financial resources …	___ are well-planned and enough for my needs	___ uncertain or inadequate to meet my needs
ADD UP →	_____	_____
	A majority of checks in this column indicates readiness to move forward with this career.	A majority of checks in this column shows a need to work on the Lifestyle Action Plan.

Key:

Choice B responses indicate items you may find challenging. Below, check off the activities that would be helpful in carrying out your career transition.

Items 1-3: Nurturing a healthy lifestyle and managing stress

Stress is a normal aspect of life. Stress hormones can be channeled for higher productivity and mental-emotional growth. People in many professions learn to work under the stress of frequent deadlines. The periodic stress of meeting proposal deadlines in your grant career may exacerbate health problems if you are not proactive about managing stress. If you eat, drink, smoke, or snap out under stress, those habits can be gradually extinguished by practicing new behaviors. Start building stress-reduction activities into your lifestyle so that you are prepared to relax when your proposal deadlines come up!

☐ If you have challenging health conditions that are exacerbated by stress, ask your doctor's advice about mindfulness and stress management classes. Make physical activity part of your regular routine. Start with a few minutes of walking at a comfortable pace. Build your time gradually until you can walk thirty minutes daily. When you start to feel your stress level building, replace negative stress habits (eating, drinking, smoking, snapping out) with a walk break.

☐ When it's not possible to get up from your computer and take a walk, choose a stress-reducing meditation technique to practice mental relaxation for five to ten minutes. The best methods will allow you to close your eyes and breathe deeply in relaxed position for a break from intensive thinking and writing.

Item 4: Adjusting to the work conditions of being seated for hours at a computer

Sitting for long periods while using a computer may cause pain or restlessness. You may be able to devise your own accommodations.

☐ Explore different chair levels for comfort. Try switching to other positions like sitting or standing at a counter. Many writers switch to a standing position. Hemingway wrote his novels standing up and many people now work from a treadmill or height-adjustable desk!

☐ Apply moist heat or use a chair massage pad for temporary relief.

☐ Take a quick exercise break or trip to the gym. An overall fitness workout includes cardiovascular (aerobic) exercise, strength training for all major muscle groups, and flexibility exercises. Strengthening exercises for core muscles (abdomen and low back) along with upper back and shoulders may relieve pain and enhance posture and comfort for the sitting position.

☐ See your doctor for acute or chronic pain. Be aware that the side effects of pain medications can be addictive, unhealthy, and likely to cloud your focus and mental abilities. Physical and occupational therapy may be better options for pain management. A physical therapist can provide exercises to improve the flexibility, strength, and endurance of the muscle groups causing your pain. An occupational therapist can suggest accommodation and positions better suited for seated work.

Item 5: Developing computer and technology skills

If you are uncomfortable using a computer or you do not often use one, you will need to increase your ease of use and know-how because computers and software programs are essential tools for a grant proposal writer.

☐ Try using the computer more for daily personal and household tasks such as researching interesting questions on the Internet, writing correspondence, and simple budget making. You can also purchase books, print manuals and see online tutorials with step-by-step instructions for advanced functions.

☐ Attend classes that offer basic skills in computer use, Internet, word processing (MS Word), and spreadsheets (MS Excel). Free or low-cost continuing education classes are offered at libraries, job centers, senior centers, high schools, and community colleges. Keep in mind, you can also learn a great deal from computer-savvy family members.

☐ Check out www.TechSoup.org to become familiar with the latest non-profit technology issues. Many nonprofit agencies are using earlier generations of Microsoft Word and Excel software.

Items 6-8: Getting support to work with deadlines

It will be crucial to obtain the support of your family and friends for the periodic demands of grant proposal writing. You can make this lifestyle change through mutual support. Don't forget to help them feel good about contributing to your success.

☐ Hold a family meeting to talk and plan together. Share your aspirations and the reasons why you are attracted to this field. Describe how your decision to become a grant writer may impact them. Let them know that you will probably need some extra breathing space when you are distracted or stressed by a project deadline. You might have to ask them to be flexible with family commitments. Listen and ask for feedback.

☐ When working from a home office, be sure to write your "work time schedule" into a household calendar.

☐ If you are caring for school-age children: (a) respond to their need for a concrete routine by making a written schedule to post and follow on Deadline Day; (b) ask everyone to add a "job" they can do to help the family get through Deadline Day with less stress; and (c) arrange for extra help to entertain or care for young children so that you can work without distraction.

☐ The arrangement needs to feel mutually beneficial and not a one-way street. Immediately following every deadline placed on the calendar, schedule special times to reconnect with loved ones.

☐ When you win a grant award, celebrate with the people who supported you. They are partly responsible for your success—so thank them and tell them how the grant money will be used. Explain that their help will have contributed to getting the project off the ground.

Items 9-10: Assessing entrepreneurial and financial needs

Your personal and family financial situation is one of the most important factors to consider when deciding whether to enter the grants profession through self-employment or in a salaried position. This choice is important when finances are a special concern. The following aspects of your financial situation should be carefully examined.

For each item below, check the answer (A or B) that is most true for you.

Financial Assessment:	Choice A	Choice B
1. My total monthly income …	___ exceeds my expenses	___ barely meets my expenses
2. My debt …	___ is <u>not</u> a limiting factor in my life choices	___ is a limiting factor in my life choices
3. My health care coverage …	___ is adequate for my needs	___ is inadequate for my needs
4. My cash reserve …	___ has a cushion of 6 or more months of living expenses	___ has less than 3 months of living expenses
5. Business start-up funding …	___ is available if needed	___ is not available
6. My office at home …	___ has adequate space and basic equipment	___ has little or no work space or basic equipment
ADD UP →	_____	_____
	A majority of checks in this column indicates possible entry into the career as a freelancer / independent contractor.	A majority of checks in this column indicates possible entry into the career as a salaried employee.

Here are some basic financial activities and good practices.

☐ Make an average monthly personal and household budget so that you are prepared to take a "no nonsense" approach to bottom-line income and expenses, and cash reserves.

☐ It may take several months to follow-through on your career action plan. Budget funds for your home office expenses (see Step 3), for local grant training workshops or online courses, and for grant reference materials. These items may be tax deductible. Consult with a tax advisor about your situation or request information from the IRS about the current home office tax rules.

☐ Discuss the risks and benefits of self-employment with your financial advisor and family.

☐ Freelance grant proposal writers should draft a start-up business plan and cash flow budget. Even if you intend to bootstrap (self-finance) your business and not request a bank loan, developing a start-up plan will give you a blueprint or "big picture" of revenue goals, expenses, and potential customers. See Chapter 6 to learn about freelance grant writing.

Lifestyle Action Plan

I will get ready for my grant career by making these changes:

Lifestyle Action Plan:	What I Want To Accomplish:	By When:
1. Physical activity		
2. Personal health		
3. Stress reduction		
4. Work accommodations		
5. Computer skills		
6. Family support		
7. Family communication		
8. Time flexibility		
9. Financial planning		
10. Deciding an entry point		

Completion Standard

Every grant professional starts out in this career or business with different strengths and challenges. The completion standard for this step is:

☐ You have identified lifestyle changes to help get you ready for a grant career.

☐ You are following through on your Lifestyle Action Plan.

☐ You have checked out the lifestyle topics, tips and tools at www.grantepreneur.com.

Step 3: Organize a Home Office

Rationale

Even if your first client or employer offers an office space, you will likely choose to work the longer days in a home office environment that is comfortable, convenient, and conducive to preparing proposals. Some freelance writers start out working from a laptop in coffee shops and libraries. Avoid public wi-fi to reduce the risk of hackers gaining access to confidential client files.

Career-Builders

Organize the space for your home office so that it is suitable for grant proposal writing. Here are some features to consider in choosing and arranging your space.

1. Select a location in your home that offers the best privacy, quietness, temperature control, and minimal interruptions.

2. Plan where to keep grant reference books and project files for quick access.

3. Decide where you will organize, sort, and lay out larger proposals.

4. Arrange desk near natural light augmented by adjustable lamp lighting to minimize eye strain.

5. Arrange the desk or main work surface near outlets for office equipment and computer.

6. Have options ready to adjust the room temperature (thermostat, fan, heater, air conditioner).

7. A space separated with a door or partition used principally for the business may be required for a home office tax deduction. Check with your tax advisor.

Home Office Diagram – Use the space below to design your home office layout.

Home Office Checklist

Keep your home office costs low by starting with what you have available before making new purchases. Take an inventory of your existing equipment and supplies. The most basic items are listed here. Check off what you already have, make a note of quantities or what needs to be purchased.

Basic Office Furniture and Equipment

☐ Bookcase(s) for reference books and supplies

☐ Cell phone

☐ Comfortable, adjustable chair

☐ Desktop computer with hard drive, monitor, keyboard, mouse, speakers OR a laptop computer

☐ Desk or table with lamp

- [ ] Surge protector and extension cord(s)
- [ ] File cabinet (lockable) to keep client files secure and confidential
- [ ] Landline phone (as back-up)
- [ ] Shredder
- [ ] Portable table for layout space to collate hard copies
- [ ] Printer (consider an all-in-one model with print-copy-scan-fax features)
- [ ] Software for Internet security, word processing and spreadsheets, PDF conversion, basic accounting
- [ ] Three-hole punch

Consumable Supplies

- [ ] Binder clips and paper clips (various sizes)
- [ ] Binders with index dividers and sheet protectors for organizing projects and proposals
- [ ] Business cards (freelancers may want letterhead, envelopes, and simple brochure)
- [ ] Copy paper
- [ ] Electronic storage such as portable hard drive
- [ ] Envelopes (business and catalog size)
- [ ] File folders (hanging and manila)
- [ ] Notepads
- [ ] Pens and pencils
- [ ] Planning calendar with plenty of space for task lists (see www.planner-pads.com)
- [ ] Post-It notes and flags
- [ ] Printer ink
- [ ] Rubber bands
- [ ] Scissors
- [ ] Stapler and staples
- [ ] White-out tape

Services

☐ Internet

☐ Email, fax, or eFax

☐ Cloud-based security and file back-up

Ergonomic Aids

☐ Adjustable chair

☐ Foot rest, back and seat cushion

☐ Gel type keyboard and mouse wrist cushions

☐ Ear plugs and head phones

Optional Environmental Aids

☐ Light-colored walls to reflect room lighting

☐ Soft sound (small fountain, fish tank)

☐ Small plant

☐ Inspiring or relaxing wall art

Completion Standard

☐ You have set up a home office that is quiet, comfortable, and equipped for writing grant proposals.

☐ Take a tour of a home-based grants office at www.grantepreneur.com.

Step 4: Build a Network in Your Community

Rationale

The nonprofit sector holds a universe of opportunities with thousands of organizations working on many different interests and causes that need the assistance of grant writers. The challenge is to find and connect with the people and agencies that share your interests, and will also provide you with volunteer opportunities that can further develop your grant skills and expand your project portfolio. If your grant proposals are successful, these same individuals and agencies are likely to offer testimonials, references, and employment at a later date.

Career-Builders

It is time to make decisions that will jump-start your career and lead to a job. A crucial step is to learn about the individuals and organizations working for your cause. Understanding how these are connected in your community will enable you to build a professional network.

The activities in this section will assist you in: (1) developing a mission statement; (2) finding contacts with common interest; and (3) building professional relationships with people and organizations that are a close match with your future desired work.

Develop a Professional Mission Statement

In the absence of a track record of grant awards, having a simple statement about your professional goal and motivation can be a bridge to share information and connect with people. Related volunteer experience, a resume of transferable skills, grant training, and writing samples will go a long way to engage potential employers or clients.

You might like to revisit Chapter 2 and transfer your thoughts to get started on writing a mission statement.

What do you want to do to make the world a better place? (From p. 20)

Next, break down this general statement into specifics by answering these questions:

1. **Who** *do you want to help? Describe these people in detail—consider gender, age, race, ethnicity, religion, social and economic status, special needs, etc.*

2. **What** *change do you want to work for? If you could instantly start developing a program, what would it be doing to help people?*

3. **Where** *can you start working for the change? Where are the people, organizations, and programs geographically located?*

4. **When** *can you get started? How much time can you offer?*

5. **Why** *is this social problem and cause important to you? Have you or your family experienced the problem? Is the problem prevalent in your community? Why does it matter? Staff at nonprofit agencies will want to know why you are interested in their work.*

Now, put your thoughts together.

My Mission Statement:

*I want to assist (1)*_____

*by writing grant proposals for (2)*_____

_____ *in (3)*_____.

*I want to get started as soon as possible. I can offer (4)*_____ *hours per week/month.*

*This issue really matters to me because (5)*_____

_____.

Take some time to refine your mission statement. Talk about your mission with family and friends until the words come naturally.

Every nonprofit organization has a mission statement. Building a professional network involves finding others who share your mission, passion, and cause.

Get ready for your chance to open conversations in elevators, interviews, letters, online social media sites, and on the phone, any of which could lead to grant opportunities.

Identifying People and Organizations with Your Interests

In life, and in the nonprofit sector, good work for a single cause does not exist in a vacuum but is always connected to other people. Some grant writers work with just one organization, while others work with several agencies that have shared interests, overlapping problems and causes, and similar target populations. Still other grant writers work for any and all organizations with a project need and the ability to pay for services.

The following exercise will help you to find people and organizations that share your interests:

1. Check off the program areas for which you have an interest in writing grant proposals.

2. Prioritize the list—note your strongest interest as #1.

3. Use the space below and on the next page to make a note of people and nonprofits in your community associated with each program area.

Program Interests	Contact Persons	Organizations
_____ Adolescents/Young Adults		
_____ Adults		
_____ Aging and Elderly		
_____ Animals		
_____ Arts and Humanities		
_____ Children		
_____ Community/Economic Development		
_____ Conservation/Environment		
_____ Disabilities		
_____ Diversity(GLBTQ)		
_____ Education (K-12)		
_____ Emergency/Disasters		
_____ Employment/Training/Workforce		
_____ Faith-Based/Religious		
_____ Food/Nutrition		
_____ Health/Disease Prevention/Education		
_____ Health/Physical Activity/Wellness		
_____ Higher Education		
_____ Historical Preservation		
_____ Homelessness		
_____ Housing Rehabilitation		
_____ Immigrants/International/Cultural		
_____ Literacy		
_____ Medical Healthcare		
_____ Medical Research		
_____ Men and Boys		
_____ Mental Health/Substance Use/Recovery		
_____ Minorities (Racial/Ethnic)		
_____ Poverty		
_____ Recreation, Sports, and Leisure		
_____ Veterans		
_____ Violence and Abuse Prevention		
_____ Women and Girls		

From this activity, you might realize that your passion is spread among a group of causes or that you are devoted to one particular population. You may have even more opportunities to enter the field as a freelance grant writer for several organizations. In this case, it will be important to create a broad professional network.

The ABC's of Network Building

A. **Ask** all the people you know about their social interests and volunteer experiences—share your personal mission statement, find out who resonates, and follow those leads. Ask for an introduction to the people they know with similar interests.

B. **Build** a list of people and organizations (name-title-email-phone-mailing address) that you know and have met. Organize your contacts in one place, such as in a spreadsheet, email group list, index card, file box, or notebook. Broaden the list by searching online for other organizations matching the program interests.

C. **Contact** the person in charge of grants/fundraising at these nonprofit organizations. Communicate your interests and ask for a meeting to discuss the possibility of writing grant proposals as a volunteer.

Initial contact with staff at nonprofit organizations may elicit a range of responses—from distrust (of anything that sounds like a sales pitch), to thrill (at finding anyone who resembles a grant writer), to polite rejection (when there is no posted opening for a grant writing position).

You can keep the conversation moving and open the door for a future position with statements such as:

- *"Can your fundraising department use an 'extra hand' from a volunteer grant writer?"*

- *"I am looking for practice and volunteer experience in grant writing."*

- *"I can also assist with other writing for the agency." (This will help you to learn more about the agency and prove your writing skills.)*

Be certain to carefully edit all letters, emails, and written communications. Offer to send an email with a small sample of your writing and be prepared to say how many hours you can commit. Remember to thank people for every opportunity.

Networking Action Plan

Enter the available information from your contacts in a spreadsheet program (Microsoft Office Excel), or your preferred email provider contact list. Create email groupings, or use an email software program that enables you to save time and effort by automating your contact lists and outreach messages. When using an email service (Constant Contact, MailChimp, Vertical Response, etc), be sure that you have permission from individuals to receive your email updates.

Helpful contact groups may include:

- [ ] Family, Friends, Neighbors and Acquaintances
- [ ] People at Your Place of Worship
- [ ] Past Co-Workers and Colleagues
- [ ] Local Groups for Grants, Fundraising and Nonprofits
- [ ] Business, Professional and Alumni Networking Groups
- [ ] Parent/Teacher/School/Youth Sports Organizations
- [ ] Volunteer Organizations (Fire Departments, Veteran's Groups, Women's Groups)

Start using your list to make calls, set up meetings, and stay in contact with people. Your initial objective is to let people know about your mission to write grant proposals for your cause and community, and ask to be connected with others.

Keep contacts fresh and current by connecting with individuals and organizations through online social media sites:

- [ ] Facebook (http://www.facebook.com): "Like" organizations, causes and people.
- [ ] LinkedIn (http://www.linkedin.com): Network with grant groups and nonprofit professionals to stay connected, ask questions, share leads, and stay up-to-date on informal news that may lead to employment and projects.
- [ ] Twitter (http://www.twitter.com): Follow people with similar interests; Tweet about issues with individuals and groups of people in real time; and tweet #grantchat to discuss weekly grant topics.

Completion Standard

☐ You have drafted a professional mission statement.

☐ You have developed a list and are actively contacting people and organizations to build your professional network in the nonprofit sector.

☐ You started contacting local nonprofit agencies about your interest in writing a volunteer grant proposal.

☐ See more networking topics, tips and tools at www.grantepreneur.com.

Step 5: Learn about Grant Seeking and Proposal Writing

Rationale

A basic understanding of grant seeking and grant proposal writing will prepare beginners to carry out entry-level tasks in a volunteer or paid grant position.

Career-Builders

You will find grant training workshops at many local colleges and libraries that are part of the Funding Information Network of the Foundation Center of New York. Recommended grant training organizations are listed in the Resources section. Start with an introductory or basic workshop. After landing a job, you will want to continue with more advanced studies.

The following learning objectives are taken from my Basic Grant Proposal Writing Workshop. You can utilize the checklist to guide your independent studies.

Basic Grant Proposal Writing—Learning Objectives Checklist:

- [ ] Understand the societal and philanthropic context for grant seeking.
- [ ] Understand who is eligible for grants and entities that provide grants.
- [ ] List the main steps in the grant seeking process.
- [ ] List the basic parts of a grant proposal.
- [ ] Describe the information contained in each part of a proposal.
- [ ] Understand the use of plain language and need to limit jargon in grant proposals.
- [ ] Understand the style choices and flexibility needed to write grant proposals.
- [ ] Read a sample grant proposal.
- [ ] Understand the post-award responsibilities for grant implementation and reporting.

Remember to list your grant training and professional development in your resume!

Completion Standard

☐ You have developed a fundamental understanding of grant seeking and proposal writing through independent study or workshop that covers these learning objectives.

☐ You have viewed the grant training topics, tips and tools at www.grantepreneur.com.

KATHERINE F. H. HEART

Step 6: Find a Mentor and Write a Grant Proposal

Rationale

You may think this step can be skipped if you already bring transferable skills from the corporate sector or other nonprofit positions. However, you will not be able to assess whether you actually enjoy writing proposals (and are good at it) until you write your first grant proposal and get feedback.

Grant proposals must be well planned and aligned with the agency's mission to solve an identified problem and serve constituents. Effective program planning and proposal writing is not done in isolation, but must occur through discussions with agency managers, program and fiscal staff, and the grant writer during the preparation of grant applications. The process can be complicated and you are likely to stumble or become discouraged without guidance and feedback from a mentor.

Career-Builders

The best way to go about finding a grant mentor and writing your first proposal is to identify a nonprofit organization working on your cause with an experienced staff grant professional. Volunteer to assist them in writing a grant proposal. Remember, the agency's designated grant writer may be the Executive Director, Development Director, Program Director, Board Member, or another person. If you have developed a local nonprofit network your contacts may be happy to offer a trial project.

Having a mentor in any profession is a tangible way to help you advance in your career. Working side-by-side with a grant writer who is willing to give you advice as you prepare a proposal, or shadowing and watching them work will give you an inside view of the process as it occurs in a nonprofit agency. A mentor will help you to develop appropriate written responses to grant guidelines, submit required documentation, and walk with you through the start to submission process. Grant writers who have written mostly rejected proposals should work with a mentor to strengthen their knowledge, skills and confidence.

My First Mentor and Grant Proposal

I approached the Executive Director (an experienced grant proposal writer) at a small healthcare agency where my spouse worked. I proposed a win-win situation: I tried proposal writing and they received an extra hand. I got helpful feedback on the mechanics of proposal writing. My first proposal was awarded $45,000 from two local foundations. I had a sample proposal and grant awards for my portfolio and resume. My mentor subsequently paid me for "as needed" work. I gained a career adviser, mentor and client for whom I continued working as she moved to other agencies. Over more than ten years, we collaborated on many successful proposals and built a strong professional relationship.

Completion Standard

☐ You checked out a sample mentoring agreement at www.grantepreneur.com.

☐ You have developed a basic level of skill by writing your first grant proposal with feedback from an experienced grant professional.

Step 7: Join a Group for Grant Professionals

Rationale

There is a great deal more to learn outside of basic grant writing tutorials, workshops, and your first several grant proposals. One of the best career advancement strategies is to join a national membership association for grant professionals and become involved with a local group or chapter that offers regular presentations and continuing education.

Career-Builders

Joining a national organization with a local chapter can connect you with other grant professionals and employment opportunities that you might not have known about, as well as improve credibility early in your career. You will find more experienced grant professionals who may act as mentors.

There are benefits to joining an organization. You will want to research the offerings and benefits of each group first and then decide which one is right for you. For example, you can become certified by different organizations, and each offers different benefits for a membership fee.

Deciding on a Professional Association

Explore the website below and check out the benefits and costs of joining a national membership organization. Another important consideration is the presence of a local chapter. Search the website and contact the national office for current information.

Grant Professionals Association (GPA) http://www.grantprofessionals.org

Benefits:

Costs:

Closest Local Chapter:

See the Resources Section for more national associations. If there is no nearby chapter, try these other strategies to find individuals and groups.

- [ ] Go to www.meetup.com to search for a grants group in your town.
- [ ] Internet: Google search for "grant writers in ____" (insert your city and state)
- [ ] LinkedIn: Start a profile and connect with others through one of the numerous grant groups. Start a discussion, ask for information and offer to meet with grant writers in your town!
- [ ] Attend local nonprofit events and conferences to meet other grant professionals.

Completion Standard

- [ ] You explored benefits and costs to decide on joining a professional association.
- [ ] You have checked out topics, tips, and tools for starting a grants group at www.grantepreneur.com

Step 8: Develop a Resume and Portfolio for Grants

Rationale

When transitioning from the corporate sector or another type of position, it is a good idea to revise your resume to highlight transferable and grant-related skills, and prepare a portfolio of your professional writing samples. Freelance grant writers should also consider developing a LinkedIn profile, marketing brochure or simple website to showcase your work.

Career-Builders

If your current resume does not involve any fundraising or grants experience, you may have to make some adjustments to it in order to transition into this field. Many of the skills that you already have are likely transferable and marketable to grant positions. A functional resume will enable you to highlight and lead off with related skills and experience.

Functional Resume for Grants:

✓ **Capabilities:** This is a short paragraph that makes your best case for being hired. Summarize your related skills such as grants, writing, editing, marketing, public relations, fundraising, and others. Related experience may include: writing grant proposals, business plans, marketing plans, other professional writing projects (be sure to have samples ready to show at interviews), and volunteer grant writing.

✓ **Education:** List your secondary and higher education degrees, academic honors, and awards.

✓ **Professional Development:** List any specialized training and certifications such as continuing education courses, webinars, and training seminars for writing and grant proposal writing.

✓ **Employment History:** List in reverse chronological order your employment history to date, including your job title, organization, employment dates, responsibilities, and accomplishments.

✓ **Volunteer and Advisory Experience:** List any volunteer experience related to grants, as well as any other related experience.

✓ **Writing Projects:** Compile a list of what you feel are your strongest and most relevant writing samples.

✓ **Affiliations and Memberships:** List your professional groups and organization memberships. Involvement in a grant writing group or association demonstrates your commitment to professional development.

✓ **Awarded Grants:** If you have worked on or obtained grants, list each one including: date; agency; proposal title, amount, funder, and your role.

Include the statement: **"References and writing samples are available upon request."**

Once you have completed the revision of your resume, there are a number of online directories where information from your resume may be summarized as a "profile." Post your profile on Monster.com, LinkedIn and others (see Resources section). The Grant Professionals Association (GPA) hosts a Consultant Directory for members.

Writing Samples Portfolio

In addition to a resume, employers and potential clients will want to see a sample of your writing. They will want to know the types of proposals you have written, such as foundation, corporate sponsorship, or government. They are also interested in knowing for whom you have written, and the funders that awarded grants. Your portfolio may contain grant writing projects you have written as well as other writing samples. For instance, my portfolio contains a list of awarded grants and contracted writing projects—it is similar to a creative writer's portfolio, except my writing samples are proposals.

Always be sure that you have secured written permission to display sample proposals and other "works-for-hire" in your portfolio used for interviews, or online at your website. Even though you have written a proposal entirely or in part, as an employee or independent contractor, the nonprofit organization is the owner of grant and fundraising materials aimed at private funders. Even in the case of government proposals available in the public domain, I recommend requesting permission for any display of a proposal from the grant recipient.

Online and Print Marketing Materials

If you already are a freelance writer or an independent consultant wishing to expand your services into grants, consider creating an online profile (e.g., LinkedIn), business card, and other marketing materials to publicize your availability for projects and business opportunities. View my website at www.heartresources.net for sample content.

A basic website for grant services should feature at least these main pages:

- ✓ **Home:** This is your landing page, which must entice potential clients to learn about your services. Your professional mission statement might be the lead.

- ✓ **About:** Summarize your professional background, qualifications and experience, and a few interesting personal facts that demonstrate passion for your cause.

- ✓ **Services:** Provide a list and brief description of writing services that you offer, address fees, and reiterate why agencies should hire you.

- ✓ **Portfolio or Sample Proposal:** Provide a well-edited writing sample related to grants (get permission to display an actual proposal, or develop a sample for your ideal project).

- ✓ **Contact:** Include your name, phone, and email address, and contact form so that potential clients can reach you.

Caution! You may want to use a blog-friendly software template or hosting site, which allow users to easily manage content. I would not recommend posting articles about your grant writing knowledge or experience until you have: (1) traveled the learning curve for grant competency to the experienced level; and (2) researched other grant blogs and LinkedIn postings for what might be considered useful content.

Overall, always keep your web copy clear, concise, and conversational. Online copy writing must capture and keep the attention of readers within a few seconds. This may be a little bit different than other styles you are accustomed to writing. Avoid aimless, lengthy, journal-like posts. You will want to invest in a business card to exchange at networking events.

Completion Standard

☐ You have checked out the topics, tips and tools for developing a grants resume, portfolio and website at www.grantepreneur.com

☐ You have revised your resume to describe your writing skills and experience.

☐ You have created an online profile at LinkedIn and business card to promote your availability as a grant proposal writer.

Step 9: Cultivate Grant Jobs

Rationale

In the corporate world, marketing and promotion is a "push-pull" endeavor that continuously attempts to motivate consumers into purchasing products and services. Conversely, the nonprofit sector favors a "cultivation" process in which the emphasis is on collaboration and working together. Developing relationships that lead to a grant position and/or projects is an ongoing process.

Career-Builders

Now that you have revised your resume, assembled your portfolio, and created an online profile, you have the tools to go after your first paid grant writing opportunity. By now, your professional network may be composed of colleagues from previous employment, new contacts, community groups, membership organizations, and volunteering. Following is a list of suggested "next moves" to assist you in reaching out through your network for grant positions and projects.

Networking Checklist

☐ The first important move is to *ask your contacts to inform you of grant positions and projects.*

☐ Attend local nonprofit meetings and conferences at which job postings and word-of-mouth leads come from members looking for grant writing assistance.

☐ Ask agency grant managers and established grant and fundraising consultants for an opportunity to provide casual part-time assistance with grant writing during heavy deadlines. (This is a sub-contractor arrangement, not "under the table" or on a commission basis.)

☐ Check the websites of organizations for which you would like to work. Where a grant position is not listed, write an email message or letter to the Executive Director explaining your interests and requesting an informational interview. Include your contact information and follow up with a courtesy phone call. The experience will prepare you for job interviews. Reach out to organizations that reflect your cause, and stay open to new options that might expand your scope of interests.

☐ Send a friendly "it was nice meeting you" email note to new contacts with whom you have swapped business cards. Remember to regularly check for positions through traditional methods such as local newspaper classifieds, Monster.com, Craigslist, along with niche-based websites like Idealist.org that lists national and international volunteer opportunities, nonprofit jobs, and internships. Post your profile and subscribe electronically to their job bulletins (see Resources).

Marketing your capabilities is an ongoing and necessary process, whether you are seeking employment as a grant writer for an agency or looking for freelance work. Even when I am actively writing proposals and have a full schedule of projects, I continuously attend networking events and stay in touch with prospective clients.

Completion Standard

☐ Check out grant job topics, tips and tools at www.grantepreneur.com.

☐ You have made a list of agency staff to contact for informational interviews, and started sending letters and/or email messages to arrange meetings.

☐ You have developed a network with grant writers and nonprofit professionals, and are staying in contact via local events, LinkedIn, grant writer groups, and other methods.

Step 10: Sell Your Grant-Related Skills at Interviews to Get Hired (and Re-Hired)

Rationale

There is only one step remaining in the job entry process. If you have followed through on the previous nine steps, you will have already accomplished a great deal.

- ✓ Brushed up your writing skills

- ✓ Planned any adjustments for lifestyle and finances

- ✓ Organized a home office

- ✓ Started building a network in your community

- ✓ Studied the basics of grant seeking and proposal writing

- ✓ Found a mentor to offer feedback and wrote your first grant proposal

- ✓ Connected with local grant professionals and reviewed the benefits of joining a grant association

- ✓ Revised your resume and created a portfolio for grants and writing samples

- ✓ Cultivated relationships that can lead to grant positions or projects

Your interviews and networking encounters offer opportunities to present your grant-related skills and experience. You must convince employers that you are the best solution for their grant needs. If you have worked on every necessary step, you should now be ready to schedule interviews with prospective employers or clients.

Career-Builders

As you begin going out on interviews, keep in mind that agency executives seek trustworthy individuals to hire for their agency's fundraising and grant department. Because there is a great deal of internal proprietary information, plans, and budgets for each agency's grant proposals, it is important to honestly represent your level of skill, capabilities and past performance in the grants field and related experience. A positive reputation will help to advance your grants career.

There is plenty of advice in articles and books about how job seekers can best present themselves at interviews for employment with nonprofit organizations (see Resources). At minimum, be sure to thoroughly review the job posting and agency website. Make a list of questions to ask and take notes in the interview rather than relying on memory. Utilize informational interviews for interviewing practice and to demonstrate your interest in the agency's cause and mission, engage in a full exchange of information, and explore whether each grant job is a mutual fit for you and the agency.

You are not going to win every job that you apply for—but experiencing the interview process multiple times will give you the knowledge and confidence to sell your skills and get hired for your first grant job, and to get re-hired for new positions and projects in the future.

Interview Objectives

My main goal at every interview is to find common interests and build relationships through which good work can take place. Assuming there is a potential fit, I like to "sell" a win-win-win situation that will benefit the agency and their constituents, while providing reasonable compensation for my services. This process (for salaried position or a contract for services) entails: (1) learning about the agency's specific funding needs and grant goals; (2) clearly describing my matching skill-set via resume, writing samples, experience, and references; and then (3) negotiating a mutually-agreeable salary or fee for services.

Questions to Ask at Interviews

Prior to the interview, review information about the organization's mission and programs on the website and Facebook, and if there is no annual report with a grants list, view the recent IRS Form 990 at http://www.charitynavigator.org.

- *What are the organization's grant and fundraising goals this year?*

- *What are the agency's pressing needs that might be funded by grants?*

- *Approximately what amounts need to be raised and the timeframe?*

- *Who will supervise the grant position, and do they have grants experience?*

- *Do other staff have grant management experience?*

- *How will the grant writer's job performance be measured?*

- *Who will be involved in developing grant proposal budgets?*

- *Who will manage grant implementation and reporting?*

- *Who will be tracking grants? Is tracking software used?*

- *Who will cultivate and manage relationships with funders?*

- *What additional responsibilities are there beyond grants, such as events and other fundraising tasks?*

- *What are the salary and benefits, and the expected start date?*

Completion Standard

☐ Check out "Red Flags in Entry-Level Grant Interviews" at ww.grante-preneur.com.

☐ You share your passion for the cause, interest in the agency, and present your training, skills and experience—and get hired as a grant writer.

☐ You are looking for a challenge, advancement or project with a new agency. Share your passion, interest in the agency, and present your training, skills and experience as a grant writer—and get re-hired.

☐ You are looking for ongoing freelance grant writing projects, and request to be included in any contract opportunities.

SIX

STARTING A GRANT BUSINESS

Congratulations on taking these steps to becoming a grant professional! Every new proposal presents challenges in the quest for funding. Each grant project is an opportunity to find the most appropriate matching funders, develop the best proposal, and win grants for vital programs and services. If you enjoy solving problems and achieving positive results through grant writing, then the steps described in this book will help you find positions and projects with nonprofits that are striving to win grants and have an impact in the community.

In summary, building a grant career involves bringing your passion for making a difference and writing skills to the learning curve of training and professional development, proposal writing feedback, and gaining experience by writing proposals to different funders (corporate, foundation, United Way, government). Grant writing for various organizations (sizes, types, causes) broadens your experience and strengthens competency. Upholding recognized ethical practices demonstrates good judgment and trustworthiness as a grant professional. Each awarded grant will help you to build a reputation for success in your career, cause and community. A combination of these factors along with word-of-mouth networking will help you get hired and re-hired.

Finding Grant Career and Business Success

Salaried grant professionals earn from $40,000 to over $70,000 plus benefits according to the *Salary and Benefits Survey* conducted in 2015 by the Grant Professionals Association. The GPA's *Consultant Salary and Benefits Survey* findings showed higher salaries and hourly rates for full-time and part-time consultants. Before jumping on the consulting bandwagon, you should take into account that there were reported "strong positive correlations between salary and years of experience, size of business, and degree of establishment of business."[11] The same surveys, and other

---

11 Grant Professionals Association, *Salary & Benefits Survey Results and Consultant Salary & Benefits Survey Results* (June 16, 2015).

ɪrces discussed in Chapter Three, indicate significant regional differences in salaries likely due to standard of living, market for grant services, and location near major metro areas. In my experience, established grant consultants and businesses have "staying power" and financial success because the owners are strong entrepreneurs. They have managed to navigate two learning curves, in both grants and business, within the competitive field of grant professional services.

Benefits of a Grant Business

After a few years of freelance grant writing and building a track record of successful grants, I launched my company, Heart Resources, LLC. Over the past ten years, it has grown into an established mission-driven grant specialty company in Western Pennsylvania. It has been rewarding to work with over thirty-five local and national organizations. Besides serving as an independent grant contractor, other roles have included: employer for freelance grant writers; sub-contractor for other consultants; development writer; grant manager; grant reviewer; nationally approved grant trainer; and coach for individuals to improve their proposal writing, grant career and business.

Here are some benefits of being a Grant*epreneur*™ in my sixties!

◊   A home office and schedule that is flexible and works well with my personal and family needs.
◊   Setting my own mission, values, price structure, and working arrangements.
◊   Freedom to develop services and products that capitalize on my capabilities and expertise.
◊   Choosing projects and clients that are aligned with my cause-related interests.

◊   Able to pay myself a good salary from a socially-responsible company.
◊   Being an innovative and proactive partner with stakeholders solving community problems.
◊   Along with this freedom come the challenges of running a business charged with raising millions of grant dollars for agencies that depend upon this funding, and the public that benefits from services.

About half of all new small businesses in the U.S. survive five years or more and about one-third survives 10 years or more.[12] Thus, the 10-year survival of my grant specialty company, Heart Resources, LLC, is an important measure of success. I am a Grant*epreneur*™—a grant professional who uses entrepreneurial skills to improve grant performance and advance my cause, community and career/business. Having a grant company involves more than "making money" and profit as a business. Also contributing to longevity is a strong publicly declared brand, identity and social mission that my nonprofit clients can relate to at www. heartresources.net.

Grant*epreneur*™ Strategies for Start-Up Freelancers

There are books, workshops and blogs offering advice on how to become a successful grant proposal writer and start a grant business. This type of business has been described as high paying and profitable. To be completely honest, there is no guarantee of quick financial success for beginners. I started out in this career as a freelancer who believed that I could "bootstrap" (self-invest and gradually grow) my business by simply promoting myself as a grant writer and automatically bring an abundant, steady flow of paying clients. Especially during the Great Recession, I discovered that it takes guts and planning to survive, and conscientious work to develop grant capabilities and marketable services while earning a living within a small business model. Yes, a grants business can become profitable once you gain the competencies, track record, and business skills to deliver the needed services to your clients at a competitive price.

I want to encourage passion for both grants and social entrepreneurship. I would highly recommend careful planning and the following strategies for anyone who wants to start pursuing grant projects as a freelancer—especially if you have little or no experience in the grants profession or small business.

Strategy #1: You may have decided upon a grant career and achieved success in a salaried position, and it is just as important to determine whether freelance grant contracting is the right choice. The IRS has rules for independent contractors, which have a bearing especially on filing taxes and taking home office deductions. A business is generally an activity carried on for a livelihood or in good faith to make a profit. If you do not have the intention of making money, and your proposal writing is carried out as a volunteer activity, avocation or hobby (that you do for enjoyment or community service rather than as a job), then no tax deductions for home office

12   Small Business Administration, https://www.sba.gov/sites/default/files/FAQ_March_2014_0.pdf (October 15, 2015).

expenses can be taken. You do not have to carry on full-time business activities to be considered self-employed. Having a part-time business in addition to your regular job will be considered self-employment. Example: You are employed full-time at a nonprofit agency as a program manager. You write grant proposals "on the side" to make extra money. You do the writing on your own laptop, and you get projects from word-of-mouth among friends, family and colleagues. You are likely to be considered by the IRS as a self-employed part-time grant writer who must pay self-employment tax and quarterly estimated taxes based on your projected income. These issues cannot be taken lightly. Learn more about your possible tax obligations and rules as a freelance grant writer by consulting with an accountant as you formulate a business plan.[13]

Strategy #2: Learn about fundraising laws and regulations for grant contractors in your state. If the purpose of your writing and other services is to prepare grant proposals for nonprofit organizations, many states require that you follow the same regulations as professional fundraisers. How you define, incorporate or promote your business (writing, technical writing, project development, consulting, marketing, etc) will be of less consequence than the actual services provided. You may have to pay an annual registration fee, and send contracts to the state for approval before any work can start. If you decide to submit grant proposals in another state, you must also follow that state's procedures for professional fundraisers. Typical exceptions are for volunteer or pro bono services, and when the contract involves preparing only government applications. Many states regulate contractors in various business categories. The statutes can be confusing, but the right stance is self-education[14] rather than avoidance. Noncompliance can result in significant fines. The "upside" of fundraising registration is: (1) learning about state rules designed to protect the public from unscrupulous schemes and scams; and (2) adding to your online profile and business card: "Professional Fundraising Counsel" (or your state designation) that will help your business to be recognized as credible and compliant with the law. Consult an attorney who specializes in nonprofit law to learn about how your grant business plans will be affected by state fundraising rules.

Strategy #3: The best way to "earn while you learn" is to get your first hire with a supervisor and agency that is established and experienced with grants. There is plenty to learn about all aspects of the grant seeking process and most people with no prior knowledge need a few years of daily work experience. This is the best place from which to build grant know-how because you will learn faster and become confident with feedback, prevent costly mistakes for the agency, and gain a positive

---

13   https://www.irs.gov/Individuals/Self-Employed (Visited October 15, 2015).

14   I highly recommend **State Charitable Solicitation Statutes:** *Everything You Wanted to Know But Were Afraid to Ask* at http://www.nonprofitissues.com.

track record while still in the early phase of the learning curve. As a beginner, the worst first-project situation is one in which you are solely responsible for grants at the agency. If you're unsure about freelancing versus a paid position, or whether the daily work of grant proposal writing is really your best career choice, try combining a part-time position at an agency and sub-contracting as an intern, apprentice, or associate with a grant consultant. Look for the Grant Professional Certified (GPC) credential for verified experience of a mentor or coach.

Strategy #4: To maintain a steady flow of projects, work on proposals aimed at various funders. Grant seeking takes place year-round, but private foundations have individualized due dates based upon the frequency of board meetings, while local, state and federal grant applications are due on a more regular schedule related to budget appropriations. Proposal writing is somewhat slower during summer vacation and holiday months. Another way that freelancers can prepare for schedule fluctuations is to add other services not dependent upon grant cycles (e.g., writing fundraising and marketing materials, annual reports, business proposals, and related writing assignments).

Strategy #5: When starting with a new agency contract, focus on learning about the agency quickly and delivering fast turn-around drafts to demonstrate that your services are productive and cost-effective. Income from freelance grant proposals can vary based upon your speed and work efficiency. A novice without a track record of grant wins will likely be offered a lower rate, and combined with less experience in turning around projects, may make less income. On the other hand, you may be the first choice for projects if you charge less during your learning process.

Strategy #6: Revenue from independent contracting grows as the grant proposal writer develops entrepreneurial skills and becomes more proactive in seeking projects and clients. Self-employed grant writers must be able to simultaneously manage the second learning curve of small business finances, contracting, marketing, and a pipeline of "next projects" to maintain cash flow—while completing current projects on deadline. Set aside a portion of revenues for cash reserves that will help pay for regular core expenses, survive off-peak months and unexpected project delays, and pay estimated taxes. Include a reasonable salary and time off for vacations.

Strategy #7: Small nonprofits require assistance to become ready to apply for grants. Working with a mix of different size agencies is prudent for business survival! Starting out as a proposal writer for new, grassroots, and small nonprofits sounds like a good proposition for all concerned. However, be aware that the hours and rates will be limited by the agency budget and financial solvency. Be sure to check on the tax-exempt status of all agencies, which is the required eligibility standard for grant applicants. Smaller agencies may take longer than anticipated to grow and build the capacity to develop, implement, and measure outcomes.

Strategy #8: Pay attention to world and U.S. societal changes, and monitor the ripple effects in the World of Grants in order to adjust your business plan for new demands and opportunities. Economic and political trends influence charitable giving and grant making. An example was the Great Recession when large stock market fluctuations and investment scams caused some charitable foundations to close their doors, and significantly reduced the endowments and operating reserves of nonprofit organizations. The 2008 Presidential election resulted in new priorities such as the American Recovery and Reinvestment Act that added billions of dollars in grants and contracts for the depression-bound U.S. economy. Grant priorities changed to assist unemployed citizens and expand basic safety net services, among others.

Strategy #9: Avoid unprofessional and unethical compensation practices. Mistakes in this arena can blemish your reputation in the community, create legal problems, and make it difficult to attract future clients. It might feel difficult to turn down an agency that insists on paying you "under the table" or on a commission basis, but you will be making the best decision for your future projects by focusing upon the majority of clients that will pay you a professional rate in a timely manner for your efforts. A positive reputation raises "social capital" for your future business opportunities.

Strategy #10: Make it a career goal to attain the GPC (Grant Professional Certified) credential from the Grant Professional Certification Institute. Eligibility involves meeting objective criteria: years of work in the grants field; number of funded proposals; community service; professional development; and formal education. The GPC Exam is composed of timed multiple choice and proposal writing tests. The GPC is a nationally recognized credential that confirms mastery of the knowledge and practice of grantsmanship, including broad experience in grant proposal writing for corporate, foundation and government funders. This validated credential provides a higher standard of qualification than a certificate from a training program or writing degree. Clients can be assured that you have a verified track record and practice with strict professional and ethical standards. According to the GPA Salary and Benefits Survey of 2015, grant professionals with the GPC credential have reported earning over $10,000 more than those without a GPC. Find more information at http://www.grantcredential.org. I found the effort and cost of taking the exam to be an excellent investment that pays for itself in receiving more requests for services from larger organizations that can pay higher rates.

The Final Ingredient for a Successful Grant Career and Business

A POSITIVE AND PERSISTENT ATTITUDE is the final factor for building a meaningful and financially successful grant career and business. While it may be difficult to persevere and remain confident through periodic grant rejections and other challenges of getting hired (and re-hired) as a grant proposal writer and consultant, this profession offers an exciting and rewarding journey filled with interesting people and projects that will make a difference for years to come.

Look for more grant career and business information and tools at: http://www.grantepreneur.com.

RESOURCES

Finding Nonprofit Organizations

Job Searches

You can learn about available positions at the web sites shown below. To search for this occupation, enter "grant writer." Some sites allow you to set up automatic email alerts when jobs that meet your specifications are announced. Others permit you to create a profile for prospective employers. Be sure to update your posted profiles.

Many of the following websites offer recent postings of nonprofit jobs, board openings and internships. Sign up for the free announcements. Some sites also include volunteer, freelance and consultant openings, and the ability to post your profile.

http://www.cgcareers.org/find-a-job

http://www.foundationlist.org

http://www.guru.com

http://www.idealist.org/info/Jobs

http://www.indeed.com/q-Grant-Writer-jobs.html

http://www.monster.com

http://www.foundationcenter.org/pnd/jobs

http://www.nonprofittalent.com (East and Mid-Atlantic)

http://www.simplyhired.com

Keyword Searches

The best search words to use at job sites are: "grants" and "grant writer." For location, use the city and state where you want to work.

"Your Cause" + "Nonprofit Agencies" + "Your Town."

Search "wikipedia" + "non-profit organizations" to see the lengthy list and types of agencies at this site. Explore the web sites of agencies that work on causes, problems, needs, or populations with which you want to work.

Search "United Way" + your city to learn about the various initiatives underway in your local nonprofit community.

Go to http://www.idealist.org to find organizations that match your interests among the thousands of national and international nonprofit volunteer and career opportunities registered with this web site of Action Without Borders. Visit the Mid-Career Transitions Resource Center. Develop your own personal profile. Download a free copy of The Idealist Guide to Nonprofit Careers for Sector Switchers.

Explore these sites for general information about the nonprofit sector and philanthropy:

National Council on Nonprofit Associations at http://www.ncna.org

The Chronicle of Philanthropy at http://www.philanthropy.com

The Foundation Center of New York at http://www.foundationcenter.org.

Nonprofit Careers

Finding the Work You Love: The Essential Guide to Reinventing Your Life by Samuel Greengard AARP Books/Sterling, 2008.

I Don't Know What I Want, But I Know It's Not This: A Step-by-Step Guide to Finding Gratifying Work by Julie Jansen, Penguin Books, 2016.

Life Entrepreneurs: Ordinary People Leading Extraordinary Lives (Stories and Strategies for Integrating Life, Work and Purpose) by Christopher Gergen and Gregg Vanourek, Jossey-Bass, 2008.

StrengthsFinder 2.0 by Tom Rath, Gallup Press, 2007 (or go to: http://sf2.strengthsfinder.com)

The Idealist Guide to Nonprofit Careers for Sector Switchers by Steven Joiner, Action Without Borders, 2010.

The Nonprofit Career Guide by Shelly Cryer, Fieldstone Alliance, 2008.

Change Your Career: Transitioning to the Nonprofit Sector by Laura Gassner Otting, Kaplan Publishing, 2007.

Nonprofit Fundraising and Philanthropy

Effective Fundraising: Real World Strategies that Work by Ilona Bray, NOLO, 2013.

Fundraising for Dummies by John Mutz & Katherine Murray, Wiley Publishing, 2010.

Fundraising Hands-On Tactics for Nonprofit Groups by L. Peter Edles, McGraw-Hill, 1993.

Giving USA 2016: The Annual Report on Philanthropy for the Year 2015, Giving USA Foundation.

The A$K: How to Ask for Support for Your Nonprofit Cause, Creative Project, or Business Venture by Laura Fredericks, Jossey-Bass, 2010.

The Development Plan by Linda Lysakowski, John Wiley & Sons, 2007.

General Writing Skills

[Note: If it has been many years since your last English class or professional writing position, choose from these books and online courses for refreshers on the fundamentals of effective writing.]

Courses

Education2Go offers refresher writing courses at: http://www.ed2go.com.

Writer's Online Workshops offers a wide range of basic to advanced creative and technical writing courses at http://www.writersonlineworkshops.com.

Guides

Cliff Notes® Writing: Grammar, Usage, and Style Quick Review, Eggenschwiler, Biggs & Reinhardt, 3rd Ed., Wiley Publishing, Inc., 2011. (Practice writing problems at http://www.cliffnotes.com)

Effective Writing: Stunning Sentences, Powerful Paragraphs, Riveting Reports by Bruce Ross-Labron, WW. Norton, 1999.

How Not to Write: The Essential Misrules of Grammar by William Safire, W. W. Norton & Company, Inc., 2005.

Merriam-Webster's Manual for Writers & Editors, Merriam-Webster Incorporated, 1998.

Robert's Rules of Writing: 101 unconventional lessons every writer needs to know by Robert Masello, Writer's Digest Books, 2005.

Roget's Super Thesaurus, by Marc McCutcheon, Writer's Digest Books, 2003.

The Elements of Style by William Strunk Jr., 2014.

The Elements of Technical Writing (3rd Edition) by Thomas E. Pearsall and Kelli Cargile Cook, Longman Publishers, 2009.

The Gregg Reference Manual, (10th Edition) by William A. Sabin, McGraw-Hill, 2010.

The Handbook of Nonsexist Writing For Writers, Editors and Speakers by Casey Miller and Kate Swift, Harper & Row, Publishers, Inc., 2001.

Writing with Precision: How to Write So That You Cannot Possibly By Misunder-stood by Jefferson D. Bates, Penguin Books, 2000.

Grant Books

[Note: This is a sampling of the print resources available. If you are uncertain about which book to read first, go to http://www.amazon.com and get a preview by clicking on "Look Inside" to examine the table of contents and sample pages. Books about grants can be dense reading, so start with one book that closely matches your interests, or choose one of the marked introductory books(*).]

Big Time Fundraising For Today's Schools by Stanley Levinson, Corwin Press, 2007.

90 Days to Success in Grant Writing by Timothy Kachinske and Judith Kachinske, Course Technology, a part of Cengage Learning, 2010.*

Demystifying Grant Seeking: What You Really Need to Do to Get Grants by Larissa Golden Brown & Martin John Brown, Jossey-Bass, 2001.

Faith-Based Grants: Aligning Your Church to Receive Abundance by Dr. Beverly A. Browning, BBA, Inc., 2005.

Grantseeker's Budget Toolkit by James Aaron Quick & Cheryl Carter New, Wiley Nonprofit Series, 2001.

Grantseeker's Toolkit: A Comprehensive Guide to Finding Funding by Cheryl Carter New and James Aaron Quick, Wiley Nonprofit Series, 1998.

Grantsmanship: Program Planning and Proposal Writing by Norton J. Kiritz, The Grantsmanship Center Inc, 2014.

Grant Writing for Dummies (5th Edition) by Beverly Browning, Wiley, 2014.*

Grassroots Grants: An Activist's Guide to Grantseeking (2nd Edition) by Andy Robinson, Jossey-Bass, 2004.*

The Foundation Center's Guide to Proposal Writing (6th Edition), Jane C. Geever, The Foundation Center, 2012.

How to Write Fundraising Materials That Raise More Money by Tom Ahern, Emerson & Church Publishers, 2007.

How to Write Knockout Proposals: What You Must Know (and Say) to Win Funding Every Time by Joseph Barbato, Emerson & Church Publishers, 2004.

Prepare for the GPC Exam: Earn Your Grant Professional Certified Credential by Annarino, Blitch, Hay de Muga, Mitchell, Charity Channel Press, 2016.

Storytelling for Grantseekers: The Guide to Creative Nonprofit Fundraising by Cheryl A Clarke, Jossey-Bass, 2009.*

Thank You for Submitting Your Proposal: A Foundation Director Reveals What Happens Next by Martin Teitel, Emerson & Church Publishers, 2006.

The Complete Book of Grant Writing: Learn to Write Grants Like a Professional by Nancy Burke Smith and E. Gabriel Works, Sourcebooks, Inc., 2012.*

The Complete Guide to Writing Effective & Award-Winning Grants: Step-by-Step Instructions with Companion CD-ROM by Dianne Harris, Atlantic Publishing Group, 2008.*

The Complete Idiot's Guide to Grant Writing (3rd Edition) by Waddy Thompson, Alpha Books, 2011.

The Only Grant-Writing Book You'll Ever Need by Ellen Karsh & Arlen Sue Fox, Carroll & Graf Publishers, 2014.

Webster's New World Grant Writing Handbook by Sara Deming Wason, Wiley, 2004.

Winning Grants Step by Step: The Complete Workbook for Planning, Developing and Writing Successful Proposals by Mim Carlson and Tori O'Neal-McElrath, Alliance for Nonprofit Management, 2013.*

Writing for a Good Cause: The Complete Guide to Crafting Proposals and Other Persuasive Pieces for Nonprofits by Joseph Barbato & Danielle S. Furlich, Simon & Shuster, 2000.*

Grant Consulting and Business

Entrepreneurial StrengthsFinder by Jim Clifton and Sangeeta Bharadwaj Bada, Ph.D., Gallup Press, 2014.

How to Become a Grant Writing Consultant by Dr. Beverly A Browning, BBA, Inc., 2005.

Start Your Own Grant-Writing Business by Entrepreneur Press and Preethi Burkholder, 2008.

The Art of the Start 2.0 by Guy Kawasaki, Portfolio/Penguin, 2015.

The Money Book for Freelancers, Part-Timers and the Self-Employed by Joseph D'Agnese and Denise Kiernan, Three Rivers Press, 2010.

The Nonprofit Consulting Playbook by Susan Schaefer and Linda Lysakowski, Charity Channel Press, 2013.

U.S. Small Business Administration – **http***://www.sba.gov*
SBA provides counseling and training to small businesses around the country through a national network of resource partners including Small Business Development Centers, Women's Business Centers, Veteran Business Centers and SCORE.

Grant Training

 Education2Go—http://www.ed2go.com
Grants and English writing courses used by many community colleges.

Grantepreneur™*—http://www.granteprenueur.com*
Free and affordable online grant courses and coaching.

GrantStation–http://www.grantstation.com and http://www.grantstation-pathfinder.com
Provides a searchable grants database and educational webinars. PathFinder is an online tool and listing of resources.

 The Foundation Center of New York—http://www.foundationcenter.org
Courses, database subscriptions, and a list of funding announcements and jobs. The Foundation Center of New York has free funding information centers in libraries, community foundations, and other nonprofit resource centers that provide a core collection of Foundation Center publications and a variety of supplementary materials and services. Network partners can be found at: http://www.foundationcenter.org/about/locations—click on "Funding Information Network" and follow directions in the directory to find the nearest resources.

 The Grantsmanship Center Inc. (TGCI) - http://www.tgci.com.
A recognized leader in the field of grant training offering 2-5 day workshops.

National Grant Associations

American Grant Writers Association (AGWA)—http://www.agwa.us

Grant Professionals Association (GPA)—http://www.grantprofessionals.org

Grant Professionals Certification Institute (GPCI)—http://www.grantcredential.org

Grant Professionals Foundation (GPF)—http://www.grantprofessionalsfoundation.org

National Grants Management Association (NGMA)—http://www.ngma.org

Thank you for purchasing my book!

I would like to hear your story. How has <u>Grantepreneur</u>^{TM}
helped you start or improve your grant career and/or business?

<u>http://www.grantepreneur.com/contact</u>

CPSIA information can be obtained
at www.ICGtesting.com
Printed in the USA
LVOW03s0330181216
517799LV00012B/954/P